Just B.R.E.A.T.H.E. & Believe

By
Mark Rodriguez

LA Tribune Publishing

The Right of Mark Rodriguez to be identified as the
Author of the work has been asserted by her in accordance
with the Copyright Act 1988.

LA Tribune Publishing
name has been established by the LA Tribune.
All Rights Reserved.

No part of this publication may be reproduced, distributed, or transmitted in any form or by any means, including photocopying, recording, or other electronic or mechanical methods without the prior and express written permission of the author or publisher, except in the case of brief quotations embodied in critical reviews and certain other noncommercial uses permitted by copyright law.

Printed in the United States of America

ISBN-9798330394166

Copyright@2024 Mark Rodriguez

About the Author

Mark Rodriguez, a two-time double lung transplant recipient and the world's only working stonemason after lung transplants brings a message of resilience, perseverance, and great faith. Embracing a Warrior's spirit and mindset he has been able to achieve the unheard of and beat the worst of odds.

By choosing to always fight and never quit he has removed losing from the equation. Warriors don't lose because we always fight.

He lives by the words THE ONLY TIME YOU TRULY LOSE IN LIFE IS WHEN YOU QUIT THERE IS NO COMING BACK FROM THAT.

He has come back from three deathbeds, two transplants, even death on the operating table, and the darkest places he has ever seen to return to his craft and career.

He is now an author, international speaker, and transformational empowerment coach and he is here to tell you IF HE CAN DO THIS EVERYBODY CAN DO IT WHATEVER THEIR IT IS.

Dedication

I dedicate this book to my Parents Bobby and Imelda Rodriguez as well as my Brother Ronnie Rodriguez all worthy Warriors. My Momma and Dad always encouraged me to write since a series of letters I wrote them starting in my formative years to young adulthood. After my diagnosis I began writing as a creative outlet and we had many enjoyable times as I would read to them what I wrote. I'll never forget their encouraging words and their belief in me.

I started writing this book in October of 2021 and I quickly realized how much healing I truly needed. It sparked a whole new journey of transformation.

My Dad passed in 2014 and my Momma in 2023 of different forms of cancer. I know they will enjoy it together.

My Parents

Ronnie my Brother

My Brother Ronnie was always the one I wanted to be like. He was so good at everything, and he made it all look easy. He was as cool as they come and didn't hate on anybody or anything. I never heard him use that word. I followed him in many ways but the biggest was in our career paths. He was one of the greatest Stonemasons I've ever learned from. He was a true Master. He could make the rocks do whatever he said to do. On Christmas Day 2023 he passed from silicosis fibrosis and some heart complications. He returned home to the LORD as a Warrior and nothing less. When I told him about the book project he said, "I do not read much Mark, but I can't wait to read this." Now you can enjoy it with Momma and Dad, and my baby Brother. If it wasn't for these three people being what they were in my life I know I would have been gone years and years ago.

Acknowledgements

I want to first thank Jesus Christ my LORD and Savior and my Heavenly Father for bringing me through all my worst days because they could have been my last one. My Mom and Dad for teaching me about the importance of a relationship with God and Jesus and for perseverance through adversity to discover our greatest talents and gifts because I did not quit and embraced my Warrior mindset and spirit at the most critical times in my life.

To my Donors for fighting to stay alive long enough to save people from death by giving them life as your last act on Earth. It does not get any bigger than that. Thank you for your commitment to a lifestyle that would ensure your ability to be a Giver of Life. I am eternally grateful for your gifts. To my Donor Families I thank you as well, for in the midst of your tragedies you remained open to and facilitated a miracle making experience.

To my family, I say thank you for what you have been to me, it has given me inspiration and motivation in so many ways.

Mari my Daughter, thank you for being so amazing through this whole journey and being more solid than any stone I have ever worked and more than most people I've dealt with. You make me proud to be a GIRL-DAD. I love you so much thank you so much for being the reason I became a real man.

Jonathan and Letitia thanks for letting me be your Dad and for many memories. I love you guys and all your awesome kiddos.

To each and every person who helped me get to this day with my whole heart. I say thank you for your prayers, love, and support.

Thank you to all the staff at Capital High School who in 2015 donated their sick hours and personal time to me to help me out when I had to leave my job at the school. I will never forget that. Thank you.

To the amazing team at St. Joseph's in Phoenix, Arizona I cannot thank you all enough for never quitting on me and always fighting to give me the best care. St. Joe's you are #1 in the country for many reasons. The most important one being you never quit. I am blessed to be in your care and part of your success. To the previous team that did quit on me, I say, "Thank you" to you as well because without you doing that I question whether or not I would have had enough fuel to keep my fires burning hot enough to produce and forge something as amazing as what has taken place since then. Never quit on anybody if you would not quit on yourself.

To my three Respiratory Therapists Mary Ellen, Joan, and Sheryl. Thank you for being the toughest Angels of Mercy I have met. You were the strongest, most understanding, demanding yet caring RT'all at the same time.

To my Wife Sandra thank you for challenging me to be a better man without telling me how to do it, for loving me the way I have needed to be loved my entire adult life. Doing Life with you has been one of the biggest gifts that was wrapped up in that initial Gift of Life I received in 2011. You truly are a Blessing in my life. When people say I am lucky I quickly tell them, "No, I am BLESSED!" I love you BEBE!

Lastly, I want to thank a little boy and a dog. Not just any little boy or dog though. I want to thank Jax and Koto. Jax for teaching me a great deal with very few words and big love. Jax is a young boy who has an old soul, level of understanding and expressiveness that will leave you speechless and pondering life's true meaning. To Koto for teaching me so much without any words at all. He is every bit as Warrior as I am. Finding joy and happiness in each day is not easy for a dog that has lost his hind legs when he used to run like the wind. He is very much alive and still handing out lessons about keeping your life moving forward anyway we can. I love you both more than words can say, but I am sorry Koto, I love my Grandson more.

I said what I said. Always believe in yourself, if you do not nobody else ever will.

Donate life banner at mvd

Koto our Warrior Dog

My Work

Me working

Rico my Chosen Brother who inspired THE LUNG TRANSPLANT STONEMASON He passed in 2020

Me and my Wife

Work Post Transplant

Table of Contents

About the Author iii

Dedication iv

Acknowledgements vi

Foreword By Roxanne Watson xv

Introduction 1

Chapter 1: This is Where it Begins 3

Chapter 2: Pulmonary Rehab 10

Chapter 3: The Call 18

Chapter 4: Game Time 28

Chapter 5: Time to go to Work 39

Chapter 6: Meds, Meds, and More Meds 48

Chapter 7: Finding Purpose and Belonging 54

Chapter 8: A Bump in the Road or a Roadblock 62

Chapter 9: Running out of Time and Waiting 82

Chapter 10: When God says it is Time 95

Chapter 11: When will you be out of the Woods?..... 102

Chapter 12: After Beating all Odds 110

Chapter 13: Finding Your Way Without
Losing Your Mind 121

Chapter 14: Doing the Unheard of 141

Chapter 15 : Gratitude 156

Chapter 16: My Donor and Donor Family 165

Chapter 17: Enjoying the Rewards................................. 186

Chapter 18: The Who and the What 201

Chapter 19: Caregivers.. 213

Chapter 20 : Warriors.. 221

Chapter 21: Looking Back and Moving Forward....... 232

Foreword
By Roxanne Watson

As a heart transplant recipient and radio talk show host on WRCR 1700 AM NY. I am always looking for stories of love and inspiration to share on our show. One day I was scrolling through our Facebook transplant support group and I came across the "lung transplant stonemason". I immediately thought what a amazing journey it must have been to need a lung transplant with a career like that. I contacted Mark as soon as I could.

As a general rule I don't interview my guests extensively before their appearance on our show so I can experience the story as my audience does. As Mark told his story all I could keep saying was "wow" over and over you have to write the book so people can hear this remarkable journey.

I'm sure as you read this book you will also be amazed by his adventure but you will also be inspired as I was. I hope you will be moved to action and take in the lessons of love and determination shared here.

Mark could have taken his gifts and went home and out to pasture. Nobody would have blamed him but no he decided to share his journey in the hopes that you would be motivated and inspired to action. Action to live your best life full of life learning experiences from a thought leader with a story to share full of love and determination.

I hope you enjoy this journey and are inspired to take one of your own.

Roxanne Watson
MICHAELS GIFTS SHOW
WRCR1700AM NY

Introduction

After thirteen years on this journey, I was finally able to make some sense of it all. I have always known that this life is not for everyone and even the ones it is for do not make it out alive. One thing is for sure though; anyone on this journey is a warrior of the greatest magnitude. Fighting for more time is one of the most difficult battles you will ever face. We all do it one day at a time but when it is toughest, it becomes one sunset and sunrise at a time, one hour at a time.

This is the story of how I fought death, for more time and my soul, to still have a chance to make a difference in this life. Giving thanks for all those who are a part of my journey and to God for showing me repeatedly what God can do with the broken and use them as tools in his toolbox.

I am grateful for all the warriors and donors that have inspired me to get to this day. As well as those, that never gave me a chance and quit on me. But, mostly for the hardest days of this journey that have truly built me at my core and soul able to enjoy the good ones, take the bad ones head on, and further the story of how God can do what God does and the miracles that happen every day with organ donation.

Chapter 1

This is Where it Begins

The fight for my life began on October 14, 2010. I had been out of sorts the whole prior month. Coughing, dizzy spells, and the heavy breathing at work was not too good.

Let's talk about work for a minute, my work specifically. I started doing stonework when I graduated High School and continued through college on breaks and weekends. I was made for stone masonry, as I would later find out.

I was 41 years old when my disease reared its ugly head and put a stop to my life, as I knew it. I am not talking about Silicosis Fibrosis I am talking about Superman disease. The one where you think you are invincible, but you are not. Side effects are thinking you can withstand anything that comes your way. Self-care is out the window because you believe nothing can hurt you. Well, I found out the hard way to put it mildly. Thankfully, there is a cure for the debilitating disease. It is when a doctor walks into your hospital room and tells you, " Mark you are dying."

Instantly you realize you are not invincible, but you are stupid. You can be defeated because a dumbass will eventually defeat themselves. For many years when I was afflicted by this horrible disease, I never protected myself doing stonework and by the highlight of my career, I did start wearing a mask it was too late. Eventually this would turn my lungs to solid stones and my choice to operate in ignorant machismo and not proper safety would cost me everything, well almost everything. In life when you have a hard head most lessons learned come the hard way.

I was definitely not the exception. In all fairness, though, when I came up in this game if you ever tried to put on a bandana to cover your mouth and nose it was usually followed by this statement:

"IF YOU CAN'T HANDLE IT PUNK, THEN GET THE HELL OUT OF HERE!"

It was this ignorant and macho attitude that put many great stonemasons into the ground. This disease does not show itself until the end stage and by then its way past too late.

I used to come home covered in dust joking about it, drawing eyeballs on my sunglasses. I never knew there was a beast lurking in the shadows, waiting. I started coughing in September and it lasted throughout the month. It was odd being that it really was not cold or flu season.

The dizzy spells started at work and stonework jobs are an extremely bad place for those. It was becoming noticeable to those around me. On October 14, I woke up feeling horrible and breathing badly. I thought maybe it was the flu or pneumonia at worst. I went to the ER, parked, and had an awful tough time getting to the doors. Once inside the staff could see I was in distress; after taking my vitals they sent me in for an X-Ray. My oxygen at 66, I could have gone into cardiac arrest at any moment.

Within a half hour I was being admitted and was told my lungs were gone. I had 8% lung function. I was making a stone fireplace the day before, how could this be happening?

After three days in an isolation room and a negative tuberculosis test, I was sent to a regular room. Although this was good news the bad was awaiting me. As the doctor walked in, I could see in his face and eyes that something very serious was going on. He then told me, "Mark you're dying of lung disease. We don't know which one yet, but we'll have answers soon."

Then he said this, as long as I live, I will never forget how I saw the doubt in him and how hard it was for him to say, "The only thing that can save you is a lung transplant but with only 8% it is highly unlikely that you will make it that long."

I know most were expecting me to pass within days but after eight, they released me more than likely thinking they will never see me again. After three weeks, I had a follow up, then a surgical biopsy the next day. Another hospital stay and my first experience with anesthesia, chest tubes and collection boxes. As I laid there, I had my talk with Jesus and being honest I'd never felt fear like that ever in my life.

Scared of the unknown and possible, I never ever thought about the flip side. I could only think about joining a bunch of other tough guys at the cemetary. My Momma and Dad came in and my Dad asked me, "What did the doctor say?"

I sharply replied, "He said I'm dying Dad!" My Dad was a big man, all about respect, not the kind of man you snapped at. I will never forget his words that followed, "Well you better get busy then and don't waste anybody's time." And I replied, "Did you hear what I said?"

His reply, "looks like you have your mind to make up, you can give up, quit, and die like a coward or you can stand up and fight like a Warrior and see what happens. Even if you fight, you still might die, but wherever you go next, you will show up a warrior and not a quitter. I will remind you Son I never raised a quitter! So, get busy fighting or get busy dying."

My Momma followed with, "You have to give it to God, Son, He is the only one who can help you right now." And so, I did. I stood up like a warrior and started fighting and I gave it to God.

It did not take me long to decide and my second chance had begun because I was still alive. I was not going to wait for lungs for it to start, I did not even know if they would come or if I would even make it long enough. One day at a time, one sunrise and sunset at a time, one hour at a time. It got worse before it got better and then depression set in. I thought the loss of my career would kill me before the silicosis. How could this be? A massive dose of life interrupted dropped on my head, slamming me harder than any hammer I have ever struck my chisel with.

One day sitting on the couch, crying uncontrollably, I turned the T.V. on so the whole block would not hear me. ESPN was on. There was a documentary on about Earvin "Magic" Johnson. The MAGIC MAN was talking openly about his diagnosis of HIV. How it stopped everything in its tracks and all he was experiencing. It felt like he was talking directly to me.

He talked about a five-day stretch where he did not leave his bed. He did not eat, drink, shower, hardly left his bed for the restroom and was deeply depressed.

He shared the words of his wife on the fifth day. She asked, "What are you going to do, just stay in bed?"

He replied, "I'm a basketball player, that's all I am, that's all I know."

She then said to him, "That's a part of you. Not all of you. But if you don't figure it out and get out of that bed, you won't be around long enough to figure it out."

Those words hit me in a way that changed me forever. I got out of bed and started trying to get stronger any way I could. Walking in place, doing some half squats, sitting against the wall, and even using a big coffee table candle as my dumbbell. I was motivated but my reality was staring me right in the face with every movement.

With my brain going 100 miles an hour and my body failing, I had to rely on my spirit.

God makes us up of three parts. The body, mind, and spirit or soul however one looks at it. This part was the least weak of the three, so I started there. If I was giving it all to God this was the perfect place to start. I had to strengthen that fully before I could start on anything else. With the belief that the other two parts would follow. First the mind then the body.

I was extremely strong in my body before I fell ill, and that strength is what kept me going so long with this disease. My spirit and mind were weak so when my body failed that is why I hit the very bottom of the rock. The rock was on top of me.

If I could get my spirit and mind strong again the body would surely follow. There I was standing there sickly, frail, and scared looking in the mirror wondering what happened and it dawned on me how very close I was to leaving this world.

I yelled, *"EITHER GET BUSY FIGHTING OR YOU'LL BE DEAD SOON AND YOU WON'T NEED TO GET BUSY DOING ANYTHING ANYMORE."*

Chapter 2

Pulmonary Rehab

My motivation for strengthening myself quickly waned as the effects of life and breaths mass exodus from my body began taking its toll mentally and physically. My spirit was getting stronger as was my faith. With my Momma's advice when I was in the hospital, I could see these developing for me spiritually.

She told me one afternoon, "Hito, you have to give it all to God, He knows better than we do and what to do with it better than we ever could."

I took that advice and ran with it as far as I could. I finally got to a place where I was good with my reality and not scared anymore. I promised to follow without question or doubt and let God have it all.

We can't say we have faith and then ask why. Most times asking why in situations like this is pointless, useless, and frankly a huge waste of time and energy that we could use to get closer to a solution.

Me and My Mom

It was January 17th, 2011, when I began pulmonary rehabilitation with the great Mary Ellen Kaye, my first respiratory therapist. She was a Godsend, as I would quickly come to realize.

Some days she was my trainer, my counselor, my confidant, my psychiatrist, and most importantly, she became my family. My Pulmonologist Dr. Vivian Lee fought hard along with Mary Ellen to keep me alive. Reaching deep into their bag of tricks to do so and keep me going.

Dr. Lee got the ball rolling for my transplant and off we went with limited options to get to our goal. Both these incredibly strong women were a blessing to me and for the next year were a team. It was a challenge, a struggle, and a labor of love for these women. Otherwise, I would be just another statistic in the cruel world that claims so many, called Silicosisville.

I can clearly recall my first day like it was yesterday. It was cold and dreary as I got out of my truck and began my trek into the gym, to experience something like I have never had before.

All the paperwork was done, consultations, as well as baseline readings, and now it was time for the machines. I mean the stationary bike, treadmill, recumbent stair stepper. This was a humbling experience. After all, I was exhausted, drained of almost everything. I could only do 3 minutes on each machine and not productive ones I might add. A grand total of 9 minutes. It took me 15 minutes to get in there! More than likely more than 15 minutes to get back to the truck.

As I finally closed the door to my truck, I looked in the rearview mirror and asked myself, "How the hell are you going to do this?"

Tears began rolling down my face and then I heard my Momma's voice *"give it to God he knows better than we do."*

I gathered myself and promised God I would never quit or question what he is doing in my life, only fight like a faithful Warrior to the very end.

I was surrounded by older men and women also experiencing cardio, and pulmonary difficulties. You would not be able to tell by watching them work and talking with them, never feeling sorry for themselves, or complaining, just displaying their incredible will to live at an advanced age despite the medical obstacles. It was truly inspiring, and I was around some of the best people I will always know. They all became like my Aunts and Uncles genuinely interested and invested in my well-being.

These two months were extremely trying to put it mildly, they assessed me to my core and the furthest limits or so I thought at the time. As spring rolled around and new life was coming forward and the doldrums of winter past, I got a renewed inspiration thanks to the unlikeliest of sources. Neither new blooms nor spring chickens they had joy about them and unmeasured positivity that was infectious.

They work so hard every day and it felt like, "What excuse could I possibly have? If they could fight like this, then I could too."

Moreover, they were doing it, believe me. They mixed their sweat with their sweetness, sprinkled smiles everywhere instead of showing the pain and struggles.

Even with all their medical challenges, they provided a lot of healing. This was a family. This was a special place where people came needing so much but leaving with so much more than they ever thought possible. I was blessed to be here at this moment in my life. It set a great foundation going forward. It was THE CENTER FOR LIVING WELL

As the days passed, I began to feel better and stronger with a different outlook and renewed commitment. The breathing was only getting worse though as the clock was ticking. That would never change with these lungs as they were literally on their last breaths.

As we moved into May, I was scheduled for an evaluation in Colorado, and it all went well, or so I thought. The team there had concerns that I could have lymphoma, and so the entire summer I was taking cancer screenings regularly of different varieties. It was nerve racking and scary because if I had cancer there would be no transplant.

I was running out of options and time. The great Doctor Tim Lopez, an oncologist gave me his own evaluation and wrote a report to the team in Colorado, clearing me of cancer and recommending me a viable candidate for lung transplant.

I approached my R.T. Mary Ellen and let her know I was coming in five days a week and staying 2 to 2 1/2 hours each day. These were not easy workouts either. I had normal healthy people wondering if they could keep up with me. I was determined to show the doctors in Colorado that I was ready by putting on weight and muscle. They would know I did not have cancer and that I could do this. What transpired over the next few months was nothing short of amazing.

I remember for the evaluation one of the doctors asked me, "If there were lungs available right now, what would you do?"

I let him know very confidently. I would say, "What are you waiting for, I've been preparing myself for a transplant and not an evaluation. I'm ready now let's do this!"

I made up my mind that I was all in, and I would give it all I had just as I did in my basketball training for difficult seasons, just as I had my entire stonemason career. I was convinced that if I were going to die doing this, a gym would be a perfect place for it to take place, being that I spent many hours working myself to my limits and even beyond in many gyms. 2 and 1/2 hours a day five days a week. I would go through two tanks of oxygen during my workouts; they were the big ones too. At 25 liters, working out, fifteen sitting, it was becoming difficult to keep my nose from falling off my face and running away from this madness, or so I thought.

People would stop and watch and would ask, "How you are doing this?"

I would simply say "With God and 25 liters!"

I got back up to 185 pounds from 140 when I left the hospital after the surgical biopsy. I was feeling more optimistic and positive because I could see there was a chance. I could also see that with my words, my example, and my actions, I was helping people. Now I was inspiring them.

The staff kept a close eye on me because I was going so hard every day pushing myself past the limits that I thought I had. See, when being tough and courageous is all you have on your side; you use them to the fullest. The fear and doubt had passed, and I was in a new mindset.

I had myself convinced that I would be the best sick person ever, with a positive attitude and unmatched need for more time with my family, especially Mari.

Mari is my daughter and one of the strongest women I know, along with my Momma, and my wife Sandra. She was barely a teenager doing the best she could watching her Dad slowly die. Brave and courageous, she held it together better than most of the adults around at that time.

We began to talk about lung transplants and the possibilities. It was not just about dying anymore it became about living again. We watched a video of a transplant, I learned about the XVIVO procedure where the hook up lungs to oxygen in a box and wash them as they breathe, which was brought up by the doctors in Colorado and we watched a video together.

Soon she became one of the only doctors I could talk to that would not drive me crazy. Without freaking her out too much more than I already did, we talked about the realities and possibilities. The closeness that followed was what I needed more than medicine, therapies, or a course of action. To say my daughter is beyond her years is a definite understatement.

After an evaluation of cancer screenings and tons of arduous work to stay alive, I received the call that I was being listed. It was a feeling I had not experienced throughout this journey so far. I felt like I had a legitimate chance at living. I remembered the memory of that first Doctor that said I was not likely to make it long enough to be listed.

I was riding an emotional high unlike anything I had ever experienced. I turned up the intensity at the gym and I was blowing people's minds including my own. I was training for the toughest and most important game of my life. It was August 6th, 2011, and little did I know that two days later they would call back to tell me I was first on the list.

This was real, this was happening and quickly. This could happen at any time. This was it and I knew I had a chance for more time with Mari. I also had a chance to prove that I had what it took to do this.

Now when I looked in the mirror, I was saying something different. Even though I did not get to the transplant, I could see some light. I could see the mountain now; I just had to make sure to get myself to the base to begin the trek to the top. I was not going to let anything stop me from getting there and there was a whole lot trying to do just that.

For seven months before my first transplant, I would wake up in the morning and sit up. I would look to my right about 90 degrees and there it would be every morning. Death waiting.

This big black form hovering from the floor to the ceiling waiting for me to breathe my last. Staring at me with those eyes that were blacker than the form itself.

I would yell at *it "GET THE OUT HELL OF THIS HOUSE! WHO TOLD YOU IT IS OK TO HANG AROUND HERE LIKE A VULTURE WAITING FOR MY LAST BREATH? I AM NOT AFRAID OF YOU! YOU ARE A COWARD! YOU WILL NOT EVEN FIGHT ME; YOU ARE JUST WAITING UNTIL I BREATHE MY LAST AND THEN STROLL IN LIKE SOME TOUIGH GUY! I WILL NOT LOSE TO A COWARD! NOW GET THE HELL OUT OF MY HOUSE!"*

Eventually I would have to explain this behavior to my Daughter because she could hear it every morning.

When she asked, I simply said, "I am chasing death from this house it thinks it can hang around here waiting."

Chapter 3

The Call

As close as I was to death, I was experiencing things that most are not privy to. Unexpected things at times but all too real to ignore. The blacked-out cloud of death is what I call it, and when you are close to the edge, you will see it. At times it was awful, other times empowering. It was as real as anything I have looked at through these eyes in this life.

After I chased it away for the moment, I would go shower, take my Daughter to high school, and then head to the gym to do my work. On October 9th, 2011, I had the worst day throughout this journey. I felt drained, empty, and questioning what I had left in the tank, and how much longer I could continue to answer the bell in this fight. It was the worst session I had; I was down and feeling broken as I ever felt. I went home after this and sat on the couch once again. I began to cry a heavy painful sob.

Then I heard a voice say, "Do not let it be two in a row tomorrow."

I went to sleep. The sun was still out, and I did not wake up until the next morning. I woke up, turned 90 degrees to the right and there it was again. This particular morning, I did not cuss or yell.

I simply stood up and asked, "What's up, coward? Are you still here scared to fight? Beat it loser you'll not be winning today."

I kind of chuckled as I headed up the stairs, only to get a reminder of my reality. Out of breath, my teeth would start hurting. Then my jaw would tighten up as if someone were drilling a screw into the bone. This would happen several times a day. I dropped off Mari and told her, "I love you," then proceeded to the hospital.

As I was walking in, I was focused and determined to not let it be two in a row. About 30 minutes in, I realized I was killing my workout so I turned it up a few notches, just to see what would happen. The workout only got better from there until it ended abruptly.

I was sitting on the bench in between sets when the gym trainer Ed walked up and asked, "What's up Mark?"

I said, "Not much Bro, just getting after it," and then my phone rang.

It said "unknown" like it always did when the transplant center called. I answered it and it was the transparent coordinator. This call was different though. No small talk. No greetings. It went straight to "Where are you?"

I told her I was working out at the hospital gym. She then asked, "Are you sitting down?"

I replied "yes."

She then said quickly, "Good. Listen up; we have a match for you. Get to the airport a Medical Jet will be waiting" Then she asked, "Did you hear me?"

I answered "Yes, but I can't talk right now."

Then she said, "Good. Just listen then."

She asked when I last ate. I told her I ate fruit earlier in the morning. Then here comes her list of what not to do.

"Don't speed or take yellow lights, wear your seat belt, don't use the phone while driving, don't panic, stay focused, we are almost there Mark."

I then said, "This is what we've been working so hard for, to get to this day."

It had been a yearlong fight, but that first doctor was about to be proven wrong, because I did make it even with everything I was up against.

I was sitting there in shock and Ed asked me, "Are you alright Bro?"

I told him in an incredibly soft childlike voice "I just got the call."

He asked nonchalantly "What call?"

I told him, "FROM THE TRANSPLANT CENTER!"

When this clicked, He helped me over to the area where they take vitals and sat me down. He went to get Mary Ellen from the office.

I heard a yell. She came out of the office quickly. It freaked me out a little because she kept screaming "OH MY GOD. OH MY GOD!"

With both hands on her head. She yelled, "Let's get vitals and get him out of here!" and that is exactly what they did.

They brought a wheelchair not to risk anything happening. This place was buzzing as the news spread. People were nervous and excited, but smiles were plenty.

As Mary Ellen was rolling me down the hall, I was thanking her for getting me there. We got to the front door going outside, I heard my name being called, and it was Helen and Carmen.

These women had become great friends throughout this process, and I love them dearly. I will never forget my gym family as I was leaving the gym. They were standing all together, screaming well-wishes with tears in their eyes.

As I drove away, I felt so much, I felt so much love and it hit me I made it to the day few gave me a chance to. The tears of joy began rolling down my face; it was all happening so fast.

The bonds I made doing this daily routine of preparing myself for this life-saving event were huge and exactly what I needed. They were all angels in my eyes helping me down this difficult and almost impossible road. They were invested in me, and I had great support. They knew all I went through, and I will always have so much love for them all.

Before I hit the road, I called my Momma, my Dad, and Mari. People close to me gathered at the house as I prepared to leave. I had my bag packed but I double-checked it anyway. I was nervous admittedly. Then the averted tragedy took place.

I went into the garage to fill up my portable unit with liquid oxygen. I hooked it up and went back inside. I walked back into the house and was bombarded with what seemed like a thousand questions at once. I forgot about the oxygen and by the time I remembered it, the tank was full and the valve on the big tank was frozen open. It was on for too long. The whole garage was filled with oxygen. I could see it rolling towards the door that the hot water was behind. I had to act fast. I could not see, so feeling my way over to the door I found the lock and threw the garage door open with a force I hadn't had in a long time. It was almost too late, but I opened it.

I was so terrified the house was about to blow up. As I walked back in, I yelled "NO MORE QUESTIONS! I ALMOST JUST BLEW US ALL UP!"

I could not see anything when I did this. It was so thick, and everyone saw the huge cloud that floated away from the house down the street. A quiet came over everyone.

My adrenaline was pumping so hard. I asked my Dad to help me with the hissing tank. We took it outside and left it there to empty itself out. We had to go we could not wait any longer. Mari and I rode with my Momma and Dad to the airport that was about 5 minutes away. I knew my daughter was scared so I tried to lighten up the mood by cracking a few jokes and taking goofy selfies with her. All the while asking God to please let me see my daughter again.

We got to the airport, and it was at a fast pace. They were preparing the jet for me to come in. As I looked around, I could see everyone crying.

I said, "God what do I do?" and God answered, "Show strength my Son."

I asked everyone to join hands, and I prayed for strength for everyone who was present and all the others who would be involved. For everyone who was involved in this at the airport and hospital and especially for the Donor and their family.

A man walked up wearing a uniform like the others and said, "It's time to go Mark."

I looked at my Momma, and she said, "They will be okay, now let's go make sure that you'll be okay!"

I said goodbye and gave hugs. I tried to reassure Mari that it would be okay and then I went to the jet. As I looked back, I could see my Dad with his arms around Mari. Both crying, with the same look on their faces.

They were the last ones I saw out the window as I taxied down the runway.

My Mom is such a faithful woman of God and trusts with everything she has. Her prayers and calming strength took me to a place of peace and positivity. The ride was quick and smooth cruising at forty thousand feet makes for a nice ride.

We got there in half an hour. It takes over six in a car. When we landed at the Regional Airport near the hospital, I could see an ambulance waiting. We exited the Medical Jet and started making our way to the Ambulance.

As we got closer, I could see the name on the ambulance. It was Pridemark.

"Are you serious? I asked my Mom, "Everything is going to be okay. I know it, Momma."

Then she asked, "How do you know?"

I told her to look at the name on the ambulance and she said "Pridemark. Are you serious?"

When I thought I was teaching my Daughter and my bonus kids the last lessons I would ever teach them, I told them many times, "Take pride in everything you do, and make sure you do a good job. Never be okay with being mediocre. Do not become the hamster in the wheel running and going nowhere.

We got to the ambulance and another round of vitals later we were on our way to the next step on my journey. One-step closer to game time. I couldn't help but think of that first Doctor though and what he said.

Sirens on and blaring! This staff was so great just like the one in the plane keeping me good from a mental standpoint.

Both the pilot and driver asked me, "Are you nervous?" I said "no," and they would say, "It's okay, it's totally natural before such a major event."

I just told them "I'm not nervous I've prepared myself for this so I'm ready." I have put the work in the gym to build myself, put work in those books Mary Ellen gave me, I am spiritually ready for battle, heck I even watched game tape of this surgery. C'mon are you serious? Yeah, I AM READY!

When I was waiting for the call almost daily, I'd be asked if I got frustrated waiting for the call to come and would always say the same thing, "No. Because every day they don't call is another day to strengthen myself and prepare for this and when God says it's time then it'll be".

While God was saying it was time for five others and me; he took an Angel by the hand and led her to us to be our perfect match and ANGELHERO.

I got to the hospital, and I was put in a room and again had my vitals checked and filled out paperwork while waiting. Soon after, I was moved to the surgical waiting area, one step closer to the goal.

Nurses, Anesthesiologists, and Doctors were in and out talking to me.

Then the Surgeon came in and said, "Hi I'm Michael" and I looked at him and said, "I know who you, I looked you up."

A bit surprised he asked, "Oh yeah what did you find?"

I answered, "Let's just say I am very confident putting my life in your hands."

An answer he was not expecting it seemed but showed him I had confidence in him. After he left, I quieted down for a bit and that is when I felt a whole flood of emotions come over me.

My Momma looked at me and asked, "Are you OK?"

With my voice breaking I said, "I keep thinking of Nana, Grandma and Grandpa, Uncle Dave and Aunt Chelo."

My Momma looked at me and said, "They're not waiting for you, they're just looking out for you to make sure you are good." At that moment, a calm came over me, and I settled into a good place.

We were laughing, joking, and telling each other I love you Bro. In high school, my Sister and I started calling her "Bro" as a joke and it took on a life of its own. It spread like wildfire and pretty soon my Momma had a 'Bro Club' and if you were in it you were good for sure.

Suddenly everyone started moving around really fast with a sense of urgency.

I looked over at my Momma and said, "I think it's going to happen soon."

Then she asked, "Why do you think that?"

I said, "Look at everyone moving around so fast, something is happening."

A few seconds passed and they came around the curtain and said, "Time to go Mark" and they wheeled me away.

After all that had taken place over the past year, we were on the verge of a miracle. Was this really happening? I was hoping it was not a dream and that everything was really happening. We were so close, but it still seemed so far away.

After the battles to stay alive, the demanding work, the Community stepping up for me, and refusing to quit. It was game time, and the team was ready to go. Prepared and calm.

"I am good right Momma?" I asked, and she replied, "Yes, you are Hito, and God has his hands all over this." Rolling down the hallway , again I think of that first Doctor and I get pumped up for gametime.

Chapter 4

Game Time

"It's time to go Mark."
That is what I heard as the curtain swung around. They put a little something in the IV and we were off.

I looked at my Momma and asked if I was good and she said I was, I closed my eyes quickly and reopened them just as fast as I looked at my Momma and said, "I love you I'll see you in a while."

Then she kissed my cheek and replied, "Yes you will Hito, I love you more," with the most beautiful smile ever.

As the tears began to roll down the same cheek she had just kissed, I could feel the cool air hitting them. Rolling down the hallway with thoughts of Doctor Doubt fueling my fight I could have gone up against any opponent at that point. It was a peaceful and powerful feeling all in one. The voices that were trying to reassure me were faint and seemed too far in the distance as we rolled down this long hallway. I looked up and it appeared as if it was narrowing or closing at the end. That was the last thing I remember.

My Dad was already on the road driving from Santa Fe with his siblings when it started, but he got there when I was still in surgery. I know that in that waiting room there was some heavy praying taking place.

Later, my Momma and Dad told me they were praying with a Black Woman whose son was getting a heart transplant at the same time. Later I would come to find out He got Michelle's heart.

It was an extremely challenging 12-hour surgery for the team for many reasons.

My disease known as Silicosis Fibrosis occurs from breathing in stone dust and Silica particulate. You breathe it in, never for it to come out.

The Surgeon later told me how he had never seen anything quite like that. He tried to remove the lungs by hand, but they would not budge. He then tried slicing them out, but the scapula would not even penetrate them so with the clock ticking he had one option he had to use, and it turned out to be a very ironic one.

He asked for the surgical hammer and chisel and began busting them out of my chest chunk by chunk. They were solid as rock. Maybe not that hard but hard enough that the hammer and chisel was the only option.

It was crazy to think I had two rocks in my chest, and they needed to be busted out. I cannot even imagine the

Surgeon saying, "Get me the surgical hammer and chisel please."

"Wait, what?"

When he told me this later, I had chills throughout my entire body. I think I even had them on my toes, my toes man!

These were my main tools as a stonemason and now they were needed to help save my life. Breaking them apart quickly and safely they worked throughout the night into the early morning. It started at 6:00 PM and concluded after 6:00 AM. Because so much invasive work had to be done in close proximity to the heart it was as touch and go as it could possibly be.

With the lungs finally removed, scraping of the Capillary Beds was needed to make sure to remove all the disease so it would not spread into the new lungs. This caused a lot of blood loss, but it is also what had to be done.

They told my parents on one of the updates "He has lost a lot of blood. We keep pumping it in, but he is losing it just as fast."

I eventually ended up having a blood transfusion of over eight liters and a human body holds a total of 11 liters.

Putting in the new lungs was probably the easier part of this whole thing. They had to be exhausted; I do not know how they could not have been.

They were amazing, that surgical team, to pull that off. At the conclusion, the Surgeon talked with my parents in detail, but they were exhausted too and relieved it went well and was over.

Remember the young man with the heart? Well almost two years later, I found out from Michelle's Mom and Dad, my DONOR PARENTS, that this young man had reached out to them and the story he told matched the same one the single mother in the waiting room shared with my parents.

They prayed together while the same ANGELHERO was saving us both. He was born with a congenital heart defect and had been sick for all his life. She was a single Mother keeping him alive. His life filled with challenges and struggles he was already battle tested. She did everything she had to make sure he would be alive for this day. Both strong and equal parts amazing Warriors.

She looked at my Momma and Dad and said, "I would do it all over again if it means my son will be okay and alive."

My parents had each other. This brave and courageous woman did it alone. Truly amazing what she had done and all they had overcome to be in this moment. These three people were all the same doing anything and everything for their sons, so they could continue life. Connections being made everywhere that night.

When they walked me on the third day, I went right past him in the ICU and said, "How are you doing Bro?"

He responded, "I'm doing pretty good."

I have to say, neither of us knew we were saved by the same ANGELHERO. On that day, God was bringing people together to witness miracles. Prayers were being answered and lives were forever being changed. I mentioned earlier they were Black and the only purpose for that is to show any and everyone that an Italian and Polish woman could save a Black and Brown mans lives with her organs. Further telling us that we are all the same because our Creator said so, We are all God's children, we are all made in his image.

What happened that night in the hospital was something special. Transplants are not a cure, they are treatment. You basically trade in one thing for three or four others. We all want time and that is what we fight for, and it never ends this fight we are in.

With everything we go through as recipients it is important to remember all our Donors went through giving us The Gift of Life as their last act on earth. For all the pain, struggles, challenges, limitations, and changes we go through it is still much better than the alternative.

This life is not for the faint of heart. It is not for the weak. It is for the strongest of Warriors only. We fight every day, every hour, every minute. My Transplant Brothers and Sisters are the strongest people I know and probably ever will be.

36 hours later, I opened my eyes and looked around the room. I was restrained and had 8 tubes coming out

of my abdomen and many other places, so that is how I knew I was in the hospital, and they had done it. I then tried to turn as much 90 degrees to my right as I could and for the first time in a long time, I did not see it. The coward finally got it.

I guess that Coward finally got the message and took off like a Loser. It was hard looking for it with the ventilator, but I knew it was gone. I could feel it gone. No lurking, hanging around, waiting like a vulture. The black cloud of Death was gone. My last breath could not come so it had to go. I have not seen it since either.

When they noticed me move, they called the doctor. They all walked in shocked to see me awake as if they were trying to figure out how I woke up so soon.

The doctor said, "I gave you enough to keep you down for a week! How can this be?" I lay there looking at them with so much amazement.

As they were looking at me, they determined I was breathing well enough, so they removed the Ventilator. It felt like they were pulling a garden hose out of my body.

When I heard my voice for some reason, I started to cry. They put me on two liters of oxygen but that quickly went away as well.

Later, that day my Surgeon walked in kind of quiet just to check in on me and to his surprise, I was awake watching the Dallas Cowboys and the New England Patriots. I remember watching Romo and Brady battle it out, and then I hear "What are you doing?"

I got scared and in a Little Mark voice I said, "Just watching the game."

"How could this be? Why wasn't I told?"

He went out of my room and was letting someone have it for not informing him right away. This man was invested in my success and me. Talented and dedicated to truly knowing how miracles work. He was humble and helpful and that is probably why he was so good.

He came back in, sat down by my bed, and started giving me the rundown in detail. I did freak out when he told me about the hammer and chisel being his only option with time being a factor.

I asked him, "How did they look?"

He looked at me with eyes wide open, laughed a little and said, "They looked like chunks of shit mixed with crushed glass! They were like brown rocks coming out piece by piece."

He told me inside they glistened under the surgical lights like crushed glass. I could not believe what I was hearing. He then told me I was really at the end of my rope, and I jokingly said, "Oh yeah? How many hands did I have on the rope Doc?"

He said, "You didn't have any you were hanging on to the strings at the end. I could feel you fighting when my hands were in your chest, so I fought with you. I could feel your will to live; I've never felt that before."

He said that had I not received this transplant I would have maybe lasted a day and a half more.

He looked at me and said, "I will never forget this surgery, this case, you Mark Rodriguez" and then I told him, "Well Doc, thanks for being a Badass."

Pondering all the things I was told, my mind was racing 1,000,000 M.P.H. and all I kept thinking was about what Doctor Doubt said when he did not think I would make it to this day, and I made it through the surgery too. I was laying there happy and smiling, even thankful for the fuel he provided, but that would quickly change.

I do not know how much later it was but as I sat up to use the bedside urinal, I felt like something moved in my chest. It felt weird, then my gown was doing a dance near my chest area, the monitors were going off.

Here comes the Team. Kind of as if something clicked on and I had no idea what was going on. The Doctor came in and she was calm and really young. The alarms were going off and everyone was helping me. I had no idea my heart rate would go up to 185 and eventually tap out at 225.

She was young but cool, calm, and collected for sure. She tells me "Don't worry, we were all expecting this."

They did a lot of invasive work near my heart, so they knew it was coming. She asked me to do a technique to slow it down without drugs. I tried it twice and it did not work. Now over two hundred beats per minute they had no choice but to give me something to temporarily stop my heart.

I signed the consent papers, and she did it. After we tried to do it twice with the manual technique to no avail; it felt like some holes were going to start blowing up. She said if they did not slow it down, I would end up back in emergency surgery.

The drug was administered to stop the heart briefly and I quickly had this look on my face, the Doctor noticed it.

She asked, "What's wrong? Are you OK?"

I asked, "Is this what it feels like when your heart stops?"

She asked, "Like what?"

"It's when your teeth start hurting really bad and then it feels like someone drilling a screw into your jawbone?"

She answered, "Yes, why?"

Then I said, "I used to feel this all the time when I would go up the stairs." She looked at me shocked and said, "You need to buy a lottery ticket when you get out of here."

I could see the heart rate coming down from 225. I was more than relieved but I was shocked to my core because I was flirting with cardiac arrest on a daily basis.

She asked me "You've been dodging bullets for a while, haven't you?" I nodded yes, then she reminded me about the lottery ticket.

Finally, the staff cleared out and I was able to rest, but I could not help but think about how many times I was that close to dropping dead. I was dodging a hell of a lot more than bullets.

About 8:00 AM, she walked in to check on me before she left, and I told her, "Thank you for staying and keeping me calm."

I said to her, "You are of great composure for someone so young in your position."

She reminded me of my Daughter who was way beyond her years and the manner in which she carried herself.

Then I asked her one final question before she left, "How long have you been here?"

She simply replied, "Only 30 hours."

"Wait what? I don't know what I would have done without you!" and then I drifted it off to sleep.

It was at this time things I could not understand, or control began to occur. Every day at 2:30, I would start crying heavily with immense sadness in my heart. Then right before sleep at that very moment you are almost there it would happen. I would see this beautiful woman in a white dress with blond hair. Standing tall, she'd be walking away, then suddenly stop, turn around, with tears rolling down her cheeks giving me a smile with eyes of the purest form. She then turned again and continued her walk. Then me hearing a name in my head repeatedly, only to find out the name of my DONOR was the one I was hearing.

When I thought I was losing my mind, I had no idea what I was on the verge of finding out about my ANGEL-HERO, Michelle. On day three, post-transplant, they started walking me, and I was blown away to be able to breathe like that again. I did not feel like I was doing it through a tiny straw anymore.

Soon I was moved to a regular room. And when the last chest tube came out, they said they needed the bed for sick people, and I had to go. I have never been happier to be kicked out of somewhere.

I walked out of the hospital eight days after a 12-hour lifesaving surgery without any oxygen. It was like none, nothing, nada! I was no longer tethered to something; I could walk freely without pushing or carrying anything.

I was so happy and grateful to God for all that had taken place. It felt like I was walking on clouds, the feeling almost as if I were in another world.

It truly is like a butterfly growing wings and flying so high and as long as desired. I was breathing fully and unlike anything I had ever felt. The freedom to just be able to fill up my lungs and empty them again is so amazing to me. I was like a kid with a new toy trying it out repeatedly and just as astonished every time I did it.

Walking through stores became like a game to see how quickly I could get the things I needed and get out of there. Even when it became something enjoyable for me, which was strange, because as a long-time athlete I absolutely despise running for training purposes. I was flying like that butterfly after leaving its cocoon.

Mark Rodriguez

Me and my Dad and Cindy my Donor Sis

Chapter 5

Time to go to Work

Recovery from surgery and rehabilitation of the body are difficult. Doing too much creates setbacks; not doing enough creates more problems.

It is a very fine line and presents itself as the perfect time to really trust, get to know your body's limits, and listen to it at all times. Just like surviving, it's one day at a time, one workout at a time, one exercise at a time.

Before my transplant, I was able to build myself to be strong enough to endure this and make recovery easier. The tricky part is knowing when to shut it down and when you are feeling good. I quickly learned that when I got to the feeling when I wanted to give more then it was shut down time. Overdoing it almost always results in a setback. It is hard to pull the reins back when you are the Stallion. It takes great discipline. You must know your limits and listen closely to everything. I am pretty sure that is why it is called Pulmonary Rehab and NOT let's pretend we are at Gold's Gym, ha ha!

It can be quite frustrating at times because there is a lot you cannot do and very little you can. In the beginning, walking is about the only thing you can do. I was so grateful for that. Nevertheless, even that must be closely monitored.

The first round of pulmonary rehab was excruciating and defeating on many days. It takes a while to start feeling thankful knowing you are accomplishing something that leads to what resembles real progress.

After the transplant, I was walking everywhere freely, of course masked up and so grateful to be able to do that again.

When I started rehab, things went quickly. In addition, here you must be patient with yourself. That was a challenge for me because I have that athlete's mentality from many days of pushing myself to the limit throughout my playing days. I pride myself on being one of the hardest workers. I was not super-fast, I could not jump out of the gym, and I was not even considered average height in college basketball. I was 5'10, 160 pounds, and always the smallest player on the court. I also was not going to let anyone outwork me either so pushing it to the limit was not new.

What was new was learning how not to do it. I was always the smallest player on the court so if I were not ready, I would be crushed. Having said that, I know I had to be the toughest. Just going to practice was not enough. I knew I had to be training when others were not, for me just to compete. Not granted the natural talent they had, I took advantage of what I did have and that was my toughness and my perseverance. My dedication and my belief in myself.

I thought I could do rehab this way, but boy was I wrong. You start out crawling and keep crawling for a good while. Eventually you start to walk but it is more of a wobble. In addition, running is way off in the distance.

Most of your focus goes to not getting down on yourself when you feel unproductive. As time passes, new things are added, and your strength progresses, as does your confidence.

My second time in rehab was different in so many ways but only one thing remained the same. I had another great Respiratory Therapist. A 44-year Veteran in the career field was exactly what I needed. Someone who has seen it all. The great Joan Balik was one of the sweetest people I had the pleasure of working with.

I am so grateful she was such a big part of my journey. Do not be fooled though, she was professional and was all about business. You do what she asks, when she asks, how she asked, if you got that you were fine, if not, good luck, I guess. Knowledgeable and dedicated, and what we all so badly needed. One of the kindest souls I have ever been blessed to cross paths with.

Overdoing would not be an issue because the boss lady was not having any of it. Her word was law in there and was not to be tested. For the first time on this entire journey, I was surrounded by lung recipients who were at all different places in the journeys. I made it a point to try to get to know everybody because it was so helpful the first time around.

All the staff were great, helping us to gain perceptive of our new normal and the road we were on that was all new to us.

Learning a new normal because our version of the old one could never be used again. We have the responsibility of finding a new normal. Constantly having to adjust things around us, sometimes daily. As time went on and my workouts began increasing, I finally began to feel the fire once more. Able to do more exercises and repetitions I thought it was time to step it up.

I developed a workout regimen that involved regaining agility, rebuilding muscle, especially our biggest ones that require the most oxygen. Specifically, our legs have to have a strong base.

With agility drills and body weight movement exercises promoting opening of the shoulders and chest I was able to progress at a higher rate. Many times, I had to mentally return to the most grueling and brutal gut check workouts from my basketball days and try to use that. Kind of tricking my mind if you will.

Doing that is helpful sometimes for moving forward. It reminded me that I was always willing to do any work for a better chance at success; I was able to channel that briefly each session. Visualization and the right frame of mind absolutely made it possible. Our minds are as powerful as we want them to be and as weak as we allow them to become.

Positive draws in the same as does negative in our thoughts, words, and eventually our actions. Recovering from a major medical event your energy is low and not easily replenished as it once was.

Wasting time is not an option but should be viewed as a precious resource and used wisely. Wasting energy is dangerous. being that we are all made-up of energy. So incredibly guilty of this, so much so, that when I fell ill, I had nothing to fight with and that is why I hit the very bottom of rock bottom. So low that the rock was on top of me.

That is where you are under the rock. It finally hit me one day as I was laying there with nothing but this horrible feeling of death lurking. I realized if I had all that I had wasted, it would be enough to fight and be all right, but I barely had enough to hang on.

In rehab, you have to be efficient and focused on where it goes. As time went on it increased quite a bit, but still not enough to be wasted ever again. Energy and Time are precious.

Throughout the process, my RT Joan recognized some things that might help others. I began mentoring pre-transplant and those that were post-transplant early on in their progress. I never had a mentor pre-transplant so I vowed to help others so they would not have to do it the same way I did.

Alone and confused I had to learn from books and videos, and Mary Ellen Kaye. She was my first RT, and I was her first transplant recipient. We learned, worked, cried, laughed, gave it all we had and fought like hell together.

After the transplant, when she came to the hospital to see me, I put on music, and we danced, and I dipped her, and then we said, "thank you" to each other.

I was so blessed with all the awesome people who fought with me and helped me through some very tough times. As long as I live, I will always be grateful for the blessings. They are to me. Leading others and teaching them my regimen was an honor and privilege. Mentoring, although very difficult, was one of the best things I did. I learned from people I was also helping. I became better as a learner for the experience and the connections I made will transcend this world. These people became my Brothers and Sisters, they became my Family.

It gave me purpose beyond what I was doing for myself and paving the road for a long journey of giving back. I met some of the most impactful people in my life and am eternally thankful for each and every one.

By the end of rehab, I was skipping rope, running, lifting weights, climbing stairs, and any other challenge

I could find. Beautiful bonds were created through helping one another. If someone were down, the rest of us would help lift him or her back up. When we were going well, the hi-high fives and hugs were everywhere.

It was a lot of hard work in these days, and mostly everything was demanding work in this phase. Except for breathing, it felt so easy and effortless. I learned from my Dad, that hard work does not guarantee your success, but it does put you in a bit better position to experience it.

Anything good or great requires hard work and if it comes easily, it probably will not last. I am so grateful I learned this because this part was nothing but hard work. You have to put it in daily or be left behind really quickly.

I always used to tell myself "Tough times don't last but tough and faithful people do!"

My Dad also taught me that discipline is not something you do with a whip, nor is it forced upon someone. Either you do what you have to, or you do not, and that is discipline. Doing it regardless of how you feel without excuses or half-assed efforts. He taught me excuses were a tool of the weak, and not to use them so as not to become that.

My Mom and Dad knew hard work and sacrifice and I am fortunate I paid attention. That is exactly what it takes to reach any goal and has benefited me countless times in my life. From basketball, to stonework, and now recovery, and rehab, I was definitely not a stranger to hard work and sacrifice and the power it generates. Some people shy away from the hard stuff or avoid it altogether, some run towards it and that is the difference between Warriors and quitters.

Never be afraid of hard work or tough times for those are what shape you into who we really are at our core and soul.

Chapter 6

Meds, Meds, and More Meds

After the transplant, everything is new, and I mean everything. Even the old things you did are new again because you must do them differently. Something brand new is taking serious amounts of meds of all kinds. The morning ones were larger than the evening dose but were still considerable.

Management or medication in the first year or so, the number goes up and down. I can recall long stretches of taking pills in the amount of 50s, 40s, and 30s. After 10 years plus for me I am around 25 or 26 depending on the day. It wreaks havoc on your life and mind, so it is important to have mentorship support to not become overwhelmed.

It took a lot of getting used to because even after brutal days on the rock pile I still would not take Tylenol much less anything else. A couple of multivitamins and that was pretty much it. I do not play with pain meds. I have seen the damage too many times, what it does and how it ruins families. You need them briefly because this kind of pain is unreal, but caution and monitoring are key to ending usage as quickly as possible. Playing catch up with your pain after lung transplant can fully mentally challenge you. The kind of pain that will drag you to your knees. Playing catch up is a dumb strategy.

One day, after a shower, dressing, brushing teeth, grooming myself, then eating, I realized I was carrying a bottle of pain pills with me everywhere. I wasn't doing that with all the other twenty plus meds I was on so why this one? It was either I was afraid of the pain, or I was being hooked like millions of unfortunate Americans and others around the world.

I decided in that moment I was not going to be a statistic, and realized I was tough enough with God on my side to handle it. Therefore, I dropped it there.

Now I know everyone is different, but please always use caution. I am not recommending my method, but it scared me. I was not overusing it, but the fact that I was carrying them all the time was a sign something was not right.

Pain management and the ability to tolerate pain are separated by a very thin line sometimes, and without proper supervision from a doctor and family, things can slip into a dark place in a short time where the costs are excessively too much to bear.

Then there is the daily regimen to get used to. It was a giant wheel of confusion for me in the beginning. It takes great discipline and mental strength to do whatever necessary to keep yourself alive, because none of it is easy. Diligence in your life is like a safety net, patience your ally.

Without all those different types working together you have no chance. With the 5% normal immune system necessary so the body will not reject the new organ, this suppression leads to infections and sickness of all types.

Because there are so many medications needed for transplants, there are side effects or causes occurring from meds. So, more meds of different kinds are needed to deal with those new side effects. Now, it's blood pressure, diabetes. Weakening bone structure, and have I mentioned the several antibiotics that are now part of my daily routine?

Oops, do not forget the Omeprazole because your stomach is going to get jacked the heck up. Do not worry, eventually it gets better, and you can trust farts a little bit more once again.

The routine of self-discipline is your new normal and becomes an old hat as some call it, and we move forward. Some stink, some taste horrible, and others can turn a stomach into a messy place. It can lead to more problems if not addressed and managed. It was now more evident than ever that water is life and the need to flush out toxins is mandatory. Many end up needing a transplant for a kidney when they do not take this seriously, as well as diet and exercise.

Figuring out how to take 40 to 50 pills is not easy but everyone has their own way, and it varies, so however you can do it more power to you. Either way you are probably going to feel and sound like a baby that drank too much milk, or a water bottle like the old school rubber ones that were a dull red. As time goes on the amount becomes less and it becomes more bearable.

I recall as I was being discharged, they handed my Dad two brown paper bags, and he asked, "What are these, groceries?" and they replied, Nope that's all of his meds."

I could not believe that eventually all of that would go in my body to keep me alive. So much to learn about them all and managing them is extremely important because any mistakes or mishaps can be costly health wise without proper medical management, you can count on having problems and rejections.

Great Pharmacists cut down on the stress that can happen with some of these specialty medications so that we could obtain them when needed. There are good ones, baed ones, and great ones. Thank you Diane M. And Diana X. For being great ones, it has made my journey so much better and less stressful.

Stress messes with everybody, even more so in transplant recipients but only if you let it, by choosing it.

My Donor was CMV positive, so I tested positive for it also.

Cytomegalovirus is the name, I think, or close to it. I am immune suppressed, so I had to get a PICC line that stayed in me long-term to deliver this medicine two times per day.

It took two hours to complete at noon, and 6:00 o'clock, every day for 100 days. It had to be kept in the fridge but administered at room temperature, and if it was not, it felt like little knives and swords going through my veins. It came in little baby bottle looking things and I needed a lot of help getting this done.

Knowing that listening to my body would be one of my main tools on this journey, especially now, I felt like I was ready for anything that would come. Little did I know I truly had no clue how unprepared I was.

Never really taking many pills, this part was one of the most difficult for me now that I needed handfuls to stay alive.

After more than a decade now, I just take them all at once and get it over with as best as I can, realizing what the alternative is.

I do not recommend anyone to do anything like I do because, well, I do things in an unconventional manner, and frankly, I am a bit weird but not like in a crazy or creepy way. We all eventually find our own way that works. In the beginning, you rely on alarms and caregivers' help.

As time passes it becomes old hat. It always helps to have that one person around you, showing their love by asking, "Did you took your pills yet?"

It all comes to you in the beginning so fast, and you have to retrain and adapt to things quickly in order to make it. This is why you have to have a great team around: your family and friends, everybody from Doctors, Coordinators, Therapists, Nurses' Aides, as well as every other employee that comes your way.

So much respect for all those that chose to help us and fight with us in our most vulnerable times. When it's all new, it takes way more than a village to navigate your way through this new world. Asking for help is smart, and being embarrassed is ridiculous.

We are Warriors not worriers! For this only serves to waste time energy and allows you to weaken yourself.

Do not worry, just pray, that is what I believe makes the difference. I have never seen the word 'stress' in the Bible, not even once. Therefore, I do not choose it for my life. I cannot say I have lived my whole life according to the Good Book. But living this way has saved myself mega tons of energy.

Chapter 7
Finding Purpose and Belonging

After falling ill, losing everything except my life and my Daughter, battling to get to transplant, through it and the recovery, we were all forced with finding our purpose for our extra time. Now we have made it to this point, we are here in the moment.

Yet still wondering where we belonged and where we are headed. Is it where we were before this massive dose of life interrupted, or are we charged with finding a new place of belonging?

After About 10 months post-transplant, I made an attempt at the unheard of, but it did not go well. I never forgot about those folks and their jobs that went south. Those ones hurt enough to make me stop. The writing on the wall was telling a lousy story that still has not set well with me.

I did not want to be making excuses. Not as a man, a recipient, or stonemason. So, I walked away broken again mostly in the heart for how it went for others. Accept failure when you have no more chances. You either walk away or be asked to. I felt awful and did not want to waste anyone else's time and money. It was a bitter pill to swallow, but I was walking away alive this time.

Admittedly, I walked away with my head down and feeling ashamed of my efforts, even though it was clearly a question of me being nowhere ready for stone masonry but not being able to say no to two jobs.

Walking away from my passion again and certainly not on my own terms. Tears rolling, realizing that my return to stonework was not an option. I had no choice but to put it down and put it away, maybe for good this time. That was an added pain that I was not expecting, and it was difficult to face.

Therefore, there I was, not knowing if I was taking the road, or if it was taking me for most days. Figuring all that out is the interesting part. However, I looked at it, no matter the angle, I was confused, lost, and scared about my future. Not to the point that it paralyzed me and prohibited me from going forward, but there definitely was a wall smack dab in the middle of my road.

I recalled the teaching of my Dad about adversity. Either you handle it, stay focused, and move forward, or stay stuck right there where it stopped you.

We have all had life knock us down as humans. Sometimes life is hard and devastating when major life events take place. We always have a choice though, fight or quit?

Even for the strongest people it is hard, but for me, I am grateful to know that God fights for me as I fight for myself. I had no idea where my choice to fight would lead me, but I was sure it was headed for more battles.

At the front of my mind was how grateful I was for all those that helped me along the way. I set out to be a helper and give back. I just let God guide me to where I could help, and that road led me all over the place for a while. Many times, feeling like I was doing no good for others or myself. I was missing signals and alerts everywhere.

Continuing exercise programs helped me get strength eventually attempting a 5K at the very hospital I was transplanted at. I was invited by a group from the respiratory therapy gym. A great group of people, all of them.

I was excited for this when I first signed up but when it was racing time, I broke my arm. 5 1/2 months after my transplant I was playing in a men's basketball league in Santa Fe against all able-bodied players. Playing ball again took me back to a time, and a very good place where I was at home and happy. Queue the tires screeching!

I was going good one game scoring my share, and then I was undercut from behind on a shot. I came down headfirst. I tried to catch myself and snapped my wrist. Now I was facing six weeks or more in a cast. They guy that did it said it was an accident but to this day I still do not know how driving your shoulders into someones lower legs from behind while they are attempting a jumpshot is an accident. Eventually I gave up trying to figure that out and started putting energy into learning forgiveness.

Two weeks after that I was sitting at a red light waiting for it to change to green and boom! I was slammed from behind and did not even see it coming. Some dumb kid changing a CD never even hitting the brakes, there were no skid marks only a puddle of Prestone coming out of his smashed-up car. My Chevy Silverado HD stopped him in his tracks. After I realized what happened in disbelief and shock, I exited my truck only to find a youngster screaming about his car that was now totaled after he bought it the day before.

"I just bought it and insured it yesterday! Hell no man!"

I was so mad I lost my entire mind. I yelled at him as I pulled up my shirt and showed my still red scar, "I just got these lungs six months ago you dumb ass!"

I was so mad, and when he could not open his door to get out because it was folded, I opened it, opened it, and kept opening it until it could not ever be closed!

He was so mad, and I just looked at him and said I did not want him to be stuck in there if a fire broke out. With the adrenaline I had going I am glad I took it out on the door and not the dumbest kid of 20 years. Right then an officer showed up and did his duties.

In talking with me, he noticed no skid marks on the road and said, "He did not even see you or else there would be skid marks."

He passed all the sobriety tests and estimated he hit me at about 50 mph. He determined he was driving HUA. I asked, "What's that?" He said, "HEAD UP ASS."

After a broken wrist, a car wreck, I was still getting off the floor. In the last six months I had a major surgery, a broken wrist, and a car wreck so at that point I was looking for anything to try and take me out. A runaway train, a drone strike, a tomahawk missile, a pterodactyl, even a gang of ninjas. I was ready for anything at that point.

The morning of the race it was raining hard, so I went down to Kmart and bought a plastic rain suit that was see through. It was hideous, but I was ready. After wrapping my arm in plastic, I had that old feeling again, like when I played college basketball. Let's do this!

It rained the whole race, but I made it to the finish line only to witness it stop a very short time after I crossed. "Oh yeah, and now it stops. Great!" While exhausted and feeling good about myself, all at the same time I realized the meaning of it all. I did it in the rain to wash away all my fears, doubts, negativity, and anything else holding me back.

It was only 3.2 miles, but it felt like I ran the New York City Marathon, and I needed rest. While many around me were inspired by the accomplishment, that made me want to do that more without losing my humility. I have never wanted to be the, *hey look at me,* person.

I then had a great chance encounter with my Surgeon and his wife. I walked up and said in a weird little certain cartoon characters voice, "Hey what's up Doc?" He looked at me a little annoyed and asked, "Do I know you?" I replied, "I hope so. You had your hands in my chest for 12 hours."

Still confused as to who I was, he asks, "What is your name?"

I said, "It is me, Doc. Mark Rodriguez." His eyes were so wide open they looked like cue balls fresh off the pool table. All I could see it was the white Part.

He then turns and looks at his wife in an astonished voice and says, "This is the man I told you about."

He then asked me, "what are you doing out here in the rain?"

I casually told him, "I just ran in the race, but I did not win or anything."

Totally freaked out and laughing at my response he asked, "What happened to your arm?"

I responded quickly, "I broke it playing in a men's basketball league game."

He asked how, so I said, as cool, and calm as can be, "Some chump took out my legs from behind because I was giving him the business."

He asked when, and I told him, "a little over a month ago" then went on to tell him that that was not all. "Also, I got slammed in a car wreck two weeks later."

Visually moved by what he heard he looked at his wife and mentioned that he knew this man was a fighter and all Warrior. He turned back to me and said, "You've inspired me this morning, like few have been able to."

I told him I would be gone if not for him and his skills and determination to fix someone so broken. I told him that he also had inspired me, and I thanked him again.

I walked away from all that with a new outlook and challenge to find my purpose. A new opportunity would be there, it would be up to me to take it or not. With newfound energy and possibilities, I set out to do more of what I accomplished on a small scale.

I was no longer feeling lost and confused, every time someone showed how I influenced him or her it motivated me to do more, as much as I could. The road took me a few places and eventually I started coaching girls' basketball while working at the high school, running the In School Suspension Program.

I also coached softball and boys' soccer at the junior varsity level. Having the chance to inspire these young adults was a blessing. I called them adults because the majority of high schoolers go through some tough stuff on a daily basis.

Reaching high schoolers is never easy but like my Dad said, "Nothing comes easy and if it does, it will not last." See, my Dad was in education and a Hall of Fame coach in New Mexico, so it was nice to connect with him like that. It gave me a glimpse of his career of turning many little boys into men and helping all his students get ready for the world.

I would never do it on his level, yet I was honored to continue his work and teachings. I loved it. I was happy and I felt like I was making a difference. I felt I was giving them tools to handle a tough world. I just hope that more of them got it than did not, but nobody ever really knows.

They did know however to not bring me excuses or weakness because of what it took me to just be in that moment.

To be clear these high schoolers did so much for me, and I am eternally grateful for that time in my life.

Chapter 8

A Bump in the Road or a Roadblock

Have you ever been doing something, and you know you are in the right place, and everything is going right? It is going good, and it just keeps getting better and then BAM! It stops dead in its tracks.

What do you do? Everybody has been riding down the road smoothly, enjoying the music and such and then you get a flat. I have heard people talk about having the worst day ever because they got a flat.

The first thing I think of is how could they be getting a flat all day? Just because you had a bad hour, does not mean you are predetermined to have another bad 23.

Goes the same for days, weeks, months, years, and so on. Sometimes in life, we like to think we know what is coming but none of us really does. Life interrupted takes place every day, somewhere, to somebody. How do we handle these events? Did they crush us, define us, or allow our real selves to step to the forefront?

Like the flat, do we let it ruin us, or do we say no more energy to anger? Do we use it to be more than we ever imagined? I had never imagined I would be the only Stonemason in the world with two double lung transplants but hey, here I am.

Yes, the tire is an example, but it could be anything. Something happens you were not expecting then you must make a choice. When life knocks you on your backside, you had better figure it out, because nobody or nothing will wait for you. It happened to me a few times.

I went from building a stone fireplace on a Friday to being told I was dying. and being admitted to the hospital Saturday morning. I will never forget that day. I was too devastated to talk about going forward.

Another time, after the transplant, the broken wrist, a car accident, the 5K, and the Transplant Games of America, I was feeling great. Healthy strong and happy. Remember that BAM I mentioned earlier? Well, it dropped, and there I was facing my very first round of rejection.

Let me tell you it was tough and interesting to say the least. I began a three-day treatment of Solumedrol. I had no idea what to expect and why I did not think anything would happen on IV Steroids is beyond me.

I had been officiating basketball games for exercise and I knew the game well. It was boys and girls leagues, adult leagues, male and female. Any league or tournament that needed help.

After my second dose late in the afternoon, I had something to eat and then I went to the gym to go call four games in a row. I was not feeling sick or anything, so I decided to do it, and I needed the money. Everything was good until the second game, the players started crying and complaining. One after another, I let them have it and bad too.

Usually, the ref has to listen to a coach or a bum, but on this night, they were listening to me. Even the non-complainers were freaked out, losing it, about to rage on these guys. All I could think of was how weak they were making themselves look and where I'd go eat after I kicked all their asses.

If somebody could have given the ref a technical, I would have been ejected, but I was in charge. No one was safe. I yelled at the kid behind the scores table because he was not talking in a big boy voice. I was even throwing hard looks over to the kids playing in the bleachers and the Mom with the crying baby.

These were real kids and babies and people, and everybody was about to get it. "How dare you cry when I am reporting a foul to the table little baby!"

I was out of control. I wanted to ask Mom if the pacifier was just for show or if she was planning to use it.

I waited by my truck for any takers for 20 minutes, and when I was alone there; it gave me time to think.

Later on, I realized I had been a major asshole because I was even talking crap to the players when they shot an air ball or messed up. That is too far. I contemplated yelling at kids and babies that were not mine. I couldn't believe how I reacted, and I felt bad and even started crying pretty hard. Then I realized I had to stop because I didn't want to choke on the triple cheeseburger I was inhaling. Steroids are crazy man!

Looking at myself, introspectively, really was a must, and an anger shock. It all got my attention, but it was brief because I was in search of more food.

I went home and isolated because hungry, crazy, psycho Ref was just a real bad look for me. No offense to all the Refs around the world.

The rejection passed and things went back to normal, but after that experience it led to learn more about these drugs and the transplant life. I realized it was time to start working out again to get my strength levels back.

The last thing I wanted was to repeat this, so I stepped it up and got back to the place I had been before. I guess that was about two years after this that I would be given the hardest of blows on this journey.

At the end of August 2015, I was 190 pounds and living life fully. My work gave me happiness and purpose. All of the high schoolers had opportunities to learn from me and I was also able to teach and inspire. The good ones, the bad ones, all of them. Most are misunderstood or misperceived by adults putting them into boxes. They are all different just like any other group. One method does not work for everybody.

I hold great memories from that time.

One morning I was running late so I was rushing. How can the person who is handing the tardy slips come in late? Not a good look.

Sitting on the bed tying my shoes I stood up too fast. I stood up and saw colors I have never seen in the crayon box, then flashes. Then I could not hear and then I could not see. I remember fainting and waking up, not really knowing where I was. I hit a big dresser right on the handle of the drawers. It hit in between my ribs. I got up in shock and came to my senses. I got up, real scared and took off to work frantically.

I knew I had hurt myself, but I had no idea how bad. It was the first couple of days of September, and it was only a few more before I could not walk any kind of distance. The kids were noticing other staff were asking questions. I also knew something was wrong. Something different from the first time.

Even though I believed I could fight this off, whatever this was, I did not have what it took to turn this one around and where it was headed. I still had a hard time thinking at that time that I would be able to make it off this part of the road. The part where I break down on the side of the road.

The principal was concerned enough to relieve me of my duties and sent me home. I was glad she did. It would have been awful for those kids had something happened there and it was about to if I stayed any longer.

It was not as if they were trying to cover their asses either, it was genuine concern. With that ticking bomb in my lung, it could have happened at any moment.

The staff at school was awesome and I will always be thankful for them. All their support, prayers and love were incredible. So many giving up their sick days to me when mine ran out. This told me that many of the people who were strangers were great people and God's helpers.

I will always be grateful for those kids too. They helped me through many rough days. I felt awful because I could not help but feel like I let them down as well as the organ donation community.

Sometime in August, I was asked to do some print work and a commercial for organ donation and I was so honored and excited. They brought a film crew to the school and took shots of me coaching kids in basketball and softball. Then we set up to do a commercial. It was a lot of fun, one of the rewards after numerous battles.

The print work is in the MVD Offices in New Mexico, and the commercial ran for Donate Life month as well. I was then chosen to do a speaking engagement for three hundred members of donor families at a function in Albuquerque.

With the first two tasks completed, there I was waiting to fulfill the third and most important one, but I felt like the clock was ticking faster than ever and I was running out of time.

I am sure they could have found a replacement with an equally incredible story because there are so many out there. But could I find one? Could I feel OK if I did not tell them the way I felt about my lungs and my Donor? I did not want to add to the failing list, so I decided I would tough it out until the speaking engagement and then I would go to the transplant center. I just had to make it a little bit longer to fulfill my obligation. I had to get there and tell all those Donor families what their loved ones mean to us as our ANGELHEROES!

They had all been through so much tragedy and grieving, and they had to know what good came out of it. Had I not made it that day it would not have been for a lack of trying or fear.

A week felt like one thousand days prior to that Friday before the event. I was ready as I could be, focused and prepared with my speech. I went to bed knowing God had all the details worked out. I woke up early at about 6:00 AM. Not because I was nervous, but because I had another commitment at 7:30 AM to a group of young basketball players. A training session arranged by their coach.

I showed up to the Community Center wanting to give them a great session but not being prepared physically. I put them through an hour and a half workout, these kids brought the energy, their fire helped my fire, and I needed that more than ever.

Now for the next step. I picked up my daughter and had breakfast and then we drove one hour to the event. On the drive from Santa Fe to Albuquerque, there was some beautiful things for the eyes to fixate on, but this morning the conversation was not on the scenery.

Very serious things were discussed, and we knew we would fight together forever, and, in that moment, I realized my Baby Girl was a Woman who is strong, smart, and has a beautiful heart. She truly is my Little Amazing.

Both of us were scared but both of us knew how strong the other was. I told her they would fix it, and I would be fine. Why did I feel like I was lying to her? I did not know if I was trying to convince her or myself.

We drove up and the park was packed and buzzing with activity. I came walking up with a T-shirt on with a picture of Michelle Stella on it. My Donor. She was my first ANGELHERO. I was looking sickly, frail, and kind of gray, because getting through that morning had taken its toll in many ways.

I was feeling awful and unsure if I could complete this task after coming so far to be in this moment. That is when I looked up and saw the Munoz family. The family of my Lung Brother Jamie who had passed away.

They honored him, as he was a great Ambassador and recipient. He was one of my first mentors. He was my teacher of all things transplant. He was my go-to person when I had questions. He was a guide when I was lost in a new world, he was my Lung Brother.

Seeing them and hugging them gave me the calm and the boost I needed all at the same time. That was how special these people are. That moment powered me to take the next steps. As I was walking on stage, I could see a school bus full of the team I helped coach. Here came the Great Coach Doyle, and the Jaguars, coming to support me. I was so ready. I was not even strong enough to hold the microphone and my small notepad at the same time, and I needed help.

For the next 12 minutes, I made them laugh, cry, feel and understand what their loved ones mean to us and their Miraculous impact. After it was over, I talked, hugged, cried, and gave thanks to as many as I could. This was why I had to honor my commitment.

Afterwards, Maria Sanders, the Director of Donor Services asked me to go have lunch with all the attendees across the street at the Zoo, because the festivities would continue there.

I had to decline.

Earlier that morning when I arrived, she saw me and was immediately alarmed because three weeks earlier we had been together at the photo and commercial shoot. I told her I was OK; I was just not feeling well that morning and she laughed at me as if I was fibbing a bit. I told her I was dropping Mari off at home and then I was driving to Denver to check into the hospital where the transplant team was expecting me. I told her I was sure I was in rejection.

I dropped off my Daughter and it was the hardest I love you good-bye ever and so was that ride to Denver.

I did not know what was waiting or if I would make it back, but I knew, it was time to fight.

Six hours later, I arrived at the ER where they were waiting. After an hour and a half of basketball training, a speaking event, and 8 hours of driving, I was walking into the ER where my day was barely beginning. I knew it was serious, but I did not fail to meet my commitments. Another failure would be revealed shortly.

My lungs were failing, and they kept me for eight days and told me I was in chronic rejection. They scheduled me to return in three weeks.

I had it firmly placed in my head that I would beat this thing or die trying. Certainly, quitting was not an option and never would be. I was working on that little spirometer gadget daily, now just trying to make it back to the next appointment. While I made it, what I was told will stay with me forever as a constant reminder of who I am and who I will allow around and with me in this fight.

I was told I was in chronic rejection, but what I was told next would light a fire under me that burns hot until this day.

"Mark, you have two months to live, so do you want us to call Hospice? There is nothing we can do for you now."

Wait! What the heck did she just say? What the heck just happened? Did they just quit on me? The thing that disgusts me and pissed me off more than anything?

Yep, that thing! I sat there still a bit floored and silent for a few seconds. One of them asked if I had heard what was said.

I replied, "Yes, I heard, but I was wondering something. Which one of you did God call?"

One of them said, "Mark this is really happening you can't be in denial. You won't beat this."

I told them, "I am not in denial, I feel myself dying more and more every day! You do not think I see and feel this. I know this is real, but if God did not call you and tell you Mark has two months then yours is an opinion, a professional one, but an opinion, nonetheless."

A silence fell over the room briefly and then I was asked again, "Do you want us to call Hospice?"

After that something happened that, I still fully do not understand but over time have come to a better understanding.

See, my last Donor was Michelle Stella who was a fierce Italian woman who did not take any crap from anybody, but she had a heart of gold and spent a lifetime helping others.

On this occasion, I believe she made her feelings clear through me about what she felt about these quitters. In this moment I looked up from the chair I was slumped in, I sat up as much as I could and then I said it.

These words in this voice.

I was born and raised in northern New Mexico, and I have a strong accent but, in this moment, I still do not know fully how it happened, but I turned into a young Robert De Niro,

I said, "I heard you, yeah, I did. I was just wondering something."

Someone asked, "What's that?"

Then I yelled back, "Let me tell you what I am going to do. I am going to fight like a Warrior with Jesus and God as my leaders, because that's what I do. And looks like you guys are ready to check out of this fight and quit, because that is what you do when you cannot handle it.

Then I added, "Why the heck are you still here you quitters!"

The doctor then said, "Come on, Mark, you don't have to be like that."

I replied, "You just quit on my life and now I'm being some kind of way. You tell me I am not worth fighting for, and then act as if I am out of line. Something wrong? Get the heck outta here. Go on you quitters and get the heck on out up here before I throw this tank at you! I then proceeded to dismantle the whole set up placing it piece by piece next to me on the chair. It was not until they heard metal sliding on metal as I removed the tank from the cart that they realized they could not catch tanks that size. I am supposed to be happy about you quitting on me, you cowards! Get the heck outta here now! If you do not want to help me, I'll find someone who will."

I left those quitters in Colorado in my rearview mirror and never looked back. I had no time or tolerance for anything weak around me, or anyone not willing to fight. I was in it 24/7 and there was no room for weakness.

For the next two months, I was determined to make it past what they had told me so I could say they were wrong. I believed that I was in rejection because I had no idea of the time bomb lurking in my left lung. It was getting worse day by day but each day I was fighting more and more.

I knew making it there and back was not guaranteed and could be my end at any time. The showers were the worst; it was scary for all 60 to 90 seconds that felt like an hour. I would get out of there shaking violently and I would have to sit on the toilet for 15 to 20 minutes to recover enough to get back to bed.

Bedridden, broken, tired, and weakened beyond measure I would lay there being grateful for making it through the toughest moments of my journey. Many days I would say thank you for making me tough, but on rare occasions, I would ask, "Why did you make me so tough, God?"

I knew one thing for sure, and that was to never let my Daughter Mari see me quit. When I saw my Dad again, he wouldn't be asking me, "Why did you quit, I never taught you that?"

I do not ever want anybody to feel the way I did when those cowards quit on me. I kept fighting with all I had left, which wasn't much, but I believed and that's what mattered most. To show her that she mattered the most and I would always fight for her until my very last breath was getting closer every day.

The calendar flipped to December, and I was past the two-month expiration date the quitters gave me and then something great happened. I talked with the transplant center in Phoenix, and they agreed to give me an evaluation. On December 5th, we drove down, and I checked in for a two-week stay.

I was too weak to do it outpatient, so I was admitted. It was an ongoing process that tested more than my body and my abilities to receive another transplant.

It tested my resilience and my willingness to do whatever it took to have more time with Mari. I was released on December 19th, feeling as if I still had a shot to keep this life going.

They agreed to help me but on one condition. I live near the hospital. If I went home, they were not interested in moving forward with me and were very clear about that.

When I got there on the fifth, the first thing they did was take an X-ray. Six hours later the nurse came in with a Coumadin pill.

I said, "I don't need those, those are for blood clots. I do not have a blood clot, are you in the right room?"

She replied, "I am, and you have one, a big one, a very dangerous one."

She gave me the medicine and then the doctor came in and said these words to me.

"Mark, you have a pulmonary embolism in your left lung. It's the size of a nickel, and it's been there for over three months."

Getting this news was a shock. Trying to do the math in my head, I was in the quitter's hospital at that time. How could they have missed that?

Something the doctors in Arizona could not help but wonder either.

I guess things are hard to find when you are not willing to look for or fight for someone. All I could think of was their diagnosis of chronic rejection. Turns out, they had a case of chronic cowardice.

Sitting in disbelief about something found initially on an X-ray, I could not help but hear those words ringing in my head like a song.

There is nothing we can do for you; do you want us to call a Hospice?

In that moment I realized I wasn't only quit on, but I was also lied to by a team that I trusted and that was more painful than anything physical I endured.

Charged with this new fuel for my life, that little voice inside me said, "Screw those losers, take it as far as you can and that's the only chance you have at showing them their lies and cowardliness had no effect on you."

I had made it three months, why not longer? Therefore, the fight took more of everything from me because there was no moving to the next level.

Survive long enough for the miracle again.

When the doctor asked me how they could have missed this, he said, "Did they do X-rays?"

I said "Yes, every day for eight days. How did you find it?"

He replied, "An X-ray! I only did the scan to see the actual size and to see how long it had been there."

The next words he said to me I will never forget because of the chill that went through my entire body.

He said, "Mark, I know you came here looking for a miracle, but I have to tell you the miracle has already happened. You should have been dead over 2 months and 25 days ago."

It was at this point that I knew I would never give up or be too exhausted to go on. I had already survived the worst, beaten the worst of odds, so I was not worried about it getting worse. I was beating odds that had not even been given this time and this was vastly different from the first time.

At least now, I understood why I felt like I had a ticking time bomb in my chest, because I did. A dangerous one and at least I knew what exactly I was up against and that is why it all felt so different.

They decided to list me, but it seemed like forever until I got the official word.

It is really strange how when you are running out of time it can drag on and on for what seems like forever.

Getting through Christmas was now the goal and then the New Year. That tells you how small the steps were. In the following weeks, they would get even smaller. Going from lightness to dark and then eventually being surprised when the clock changed hours.

So many moments where I was so close to crossing over and the battle being done. I was fighting harder and praying every chance I could but not for myself. For those that would be affected deeply by my passing and for the ANGELHERO and their family that would be coming through some difficult times of their own.

I was down to 125 pounds, and I could not walk, so my Momma would push me around in a wheelchair. I would say that she was finally the back seat driver, and we could get a laugh out of a really hard situation.

I was never this sick the first time and I felt the rope slipping out of my hands again, just trying to hold onto the last threads and strings. The glass was not half-empty or half full, all I had was a drink in there. I knew it was there though when I would need it. Being told I was being listed gave me more hope and I could see a little light down the tunnel.

On January 19, I was told I was officially listed. The light grew stronger down that tunnel and my hope for living just got a major boost.

All I could do for exercise was some light movements in the bed, and abdominal exercises. I would force myself to do them because I felt so bad, and I was so weak. I would yell at myself that I would do these exercises today one way or another. I was either going to survive or be the only one in the morgue with a six pack but make no mistake I would do these exercises today.

At this point, some of the things no one gets to see unless they are on the edge of crossing over to the next phase of their journey were happening more frequently and intensely.

I held a lot of that in because sometimes telling others made me feel like I was losing my mind. I was losing my mind from lack of oxygen, but what I was experiencing was real. It was an hour-to-hour fight at this point, being grateful for sunsets and clocks changing hours, for the little things we all take for granted.

I woke up on January 23rd and struggled to the bathroom and back to the bed. I almost fell and my Momma heard me. She came in and asked if I was ok.

I said, "I'm just really weak, Mom." She cared for me and brought me some fruit for breakfast. I ate a piece of watermelon and pineapple, and it felt like I just ran ten miles. I could not breathe. I told my Mom that I could not do it, and she took the bowl away. That day I did not get out of bed all day or night, and in that moment, I had never felt closer to death.

Laying there thinking nonstop I felt it start to happen. An unforgettable experience that had me on the verge of leaving. Laying there, I began to feel this strange sensation. I felt like I was floating away, my whole body. I panicked and grabbed the blankets. While clenching them my Daughter noticed something and asked me what was wrong. I told her that it was nothing and I thought the sheets were bunched up underneath me.

She had me sit up to fix them, but they were fine, so she laid me back down and after a minute, it happened again. I clutched the blanket fearlessly not wanting my daughter to see me die right in front of her. I held on to everything I had. She saw this and called out to my mom. "Grandma, something is wrong with my Dad, and he will not say."

My Mom came in and said I had eaten all day, so she made me some food.

Around 8:30 PM, maybe 9, she brought me a bowl of food. I was not hungry, but you do not argue with a New Mexican Momma when they are trying to feed you. Especially, my Momma, for that matter.

All I wanted was to stop this hot air balloon imitation from continuing and she was just doing what good Mommas do.

I said my prayers as I do before every meal and then dipped the spoon into the bowl. I was raising the spoon to my mouth when it happened. The phone rang. I was trying so desperately not to let my Daughter's last vision of me to be me dying, so I was fighting hard but it felt like this was the end.

It was at this point that I realized that strange feeling was my soul leaving my body. I was given my last moments, eating my last meal, taking my last breath so why was I not grateful to be with them? Mostly because I didn't want my Daughter to watch me die.

The ring of the phone stopped all of that, especially the meal. I saw it on the phone as it said unknown caller, and that is how the transplant center came up.

I put the spoon in the bowl and answered. In that moment what happened to me after seeing my imminent death being put on hold, it was heart charging. I was truly saved by the bell.

Ring ring ring and say hello, just then I hear, "Mark can you hear me?" I said YES as loud as I could with my raspy weak voice. "Get to the hospital we have your lungs!"

I was told to get the hospital immediately, that they had my lungs. I could not believe what I was hearing. No chance, no odds, yet we were off. I could see that light again and I knew it was the Championship rounds of this fight but I had no idea what was to come.

Chapter 9

Running out of Time and Waiting

When time is not on your side and you are waiting, it is a real hard place to be. On the one hand, you know the clock is ticking and it feels like it has sped up rather than slow down. Then there is waiting. Also, a tough place to be. Waiting for more time, needing an ANGELHERO and a miracle, but knowing that praying in a self-serving manner, is especially gross at a time like this.

I never prayed for lungs, but I did pray for acceptance for whatever God's Will would be. I prayed for courage, strength and understanding. I also prayed that I could still be a helper somehow, even in my current state. Waiting for an ANGELHERO to be led by the hand by God to you is different from praying for lungs.

I prayed for people and families I never met and those that would feel my passing deeply. I prayed for others fighting the same fight, and for the souls of the Warriors that had gone on before their families and me.

I do not know anyone that is self-serving that they would want death for another so they could live, but I guess anything is possible in this crazy world. The reality of organ donation though, is always amazing when something beautiful comes from a tragedy.

Accepting God's Will be done is why I felt comfortable praying, and I just kept believing it was a win-win situation. I still do. If I got the lungs great, I get more time I win. If I do not and I die. I get to go home where we all want to go someday, and that is an even bigger win. Actually, the biggest of all so, I was good either way. There would be the gift of life either way. I believe God facilitates these matches and it is on God's time.

Who am I to question what God is doing in my life? Asking why only serves to waste time that we are running out of. The truth of it is we are all running out of time because nobody has figured out how to slow it down or turn it around. Each day that passes, we have moved one more day closer to our death so make sure you are living it fully.

A life in idle or neutral is not much of a life. If you are constantly looking backwards how you can move forward? That is just it, you cannot, and that is why rearview mirrors are small, windshields are big, and life has no reverse gear. The past only serves to be grateful for and to learn from, never to be used as a means to beat ourselves up with.

Look back only for a short glance but stay focused on the road ahead. I have seen some do the "Why Me, game" you know the one. "Why me? Why does this stuff always happen to me? Why this? Why that?"

It is hard to watch and even harder to listen to. Ultimately, it will lead to the demise of the one playing that game. The Why Me Game is life sucking and exhausting 100% of the time. That is why I embraced being THE WHY NOT ME GUY. Hey if God has this much confidence in me then I better match that in myself.

For me personally I knew if I did that, it would surely be my ending. Wasting energy on hatred, anger, jealousy, revenge, doubt, and disrespect only serves to weaken a human body, mind, and soul. Failure to do what is needed to go on means total failure in the end. All these things I have learned the hard way.

When you are healthy, the waste of our precious resources goes largely unnoticed, but when sick and unable to replenish that resource as easily as we once did, that is when we see the price of our bad choices and energy placement.

When I first felt ill, I learned this the hard way. As I lay in the hospital bed after being told I was dying. I lay there in silence. I could not help but think if I had had all that energy I wasted, where I would be right now. I would have enough energy to fight this, but the reality was I did not, because of the choice I made excessively and repeatedly.

Energy truly is like a river. It flows and you never have or see that same energy or water again. So do not waste your precious resources, and God knows I have. You cannot take it back or reuse it. It has just gone downstream. Usually, it takes a hard life lesson to figure that one out. That is unfortunate because for some it comes too late.

When you are facing your death and in the middle of the fight for your life, energy placement, in addition to time management are about as important as it gets. Wasting time while running out of it is truly the highest form of self-sabotage.

You notice this when you are low on it and sick. You cannot recharge fast enough. Even if we are healthy, it is not OK. Life is too short and changes too frequently nowadays, even faster than a drop of a dime for some of us.

This was one of the most valuable lessons I learned on this journey. Guilty of this for many years, I know I still had to make some big changes in my life or I would be gone soon. Just another sad story of somebody not changing what is right in front of them knowing it is their downfall.

We either pay attention and just move forward or find another form of quitting. Refusal to change what is harmful and dangerous is another way of quitting and accepting you can never change it. You stay on that course and ride it out until the eventual consequences occur. The only thing anyone can count on being consistent is the constant change we live with. Unwillingness to change means falling to the wayside.

It is still possible when one falls ill and always one of the most important options we have. Insanity is doing the same thing over and over and expecting a different result. Change is inevitable and necessary throughout life, several times over.

In life we can either change or die, it is that simple. Everyone and every case is different, so every solution must also be in its own way. We could take a page out of the Eagle's way of life. At around 40 years their beaks, talons, and feathers are no longer useable. So they have a choice to make. Go through a very painful and difficult process that involves smashing their beak on a rock till it falls off, waiting for a new one to grow in and then use the new one to rip out the talons one by one. After the new set of talons grows in they use them to pluck out all their feathers that are no longer good for flying. When the new feathers have grown in fully it is about 150 days later and they are ready for the second half of their life. Some of us are not even willing to change the things we know are killing us but we know how to complain or make excuses. Collectively, as a people we must stop this and embrace change, the change that will lead us to our greatest version of ourselves.

When we waste energy on asking why and choosing anger about a situation, it only serves to weaken us and remove us further from the solution.

It has been said repeatedly, you get back what you put out there, that is why the world is round and spins in a circle. You exhale love and positivity; it will come back to you even stronger. If you throw rocks those will eventually smack you in the back of the head much harder than when you threw it. That is why it is so annoyingly sad to hear someone say, why me? When the rock they throw comes back around and pops them in the head, why are they always surprised?

While on the list waiting, I had plenty of time to think about my life and what it consisted of up until then. What I summarized was that yes, I had done my fair share of bad, but it did not come close to my good. I always had the ability to turn a bad situation into a positive outcome. But how would God's eyes see it?

Truth is, it would not have tipped the scales either way, but I was also in control of that. I knew I was close to leaving this place and this life back in 2010 when all this started.

I was imagining what my judgment day would be like, and in my mind, it was not good. Too many tallies on the wrong side of the Ledger are never good nor will they ever be. Therefore, I decided to start helping others when I was at my weakest because I knew time was running out to balance the scales.

I had a long way to go and a short time to get there, so I was really trying to make time like Smokey the Bandit. Sorry youngsters Google that one. As I said earlier, my selflessness started to balance out my good and bad before I left this place, but I realized quickly it was wrong. At first, I would say, OK, one more for the good side. I figured if I stopped adding to the bad and only the good side, I would be OK; then, this thing took on a life of its own.

I started out by helping others in cardiopulmonary rehab who were more advanced in age than I was. They were battling serious issues as well. With my example, approach, and words, I was able to reach others, and help them find their situations. Then it spread to people in the hospital and eventually many others outside of that setting.

I was helping people who lost jobs, houses, failed relationships, depression issues, financial issues, and family problems. Ironically, because of my illness I had experienced all of these things, so I was in a great place to help.

It was as if God were sending me all of this so I could realize that in order to receive I had to be willing to give first. It did not take me long to get the message and ask for forgiveness for my selfish reasons.

I realized I would first have to be a helper to people before it came back to me. I was totally fine with that. I was fine with that it felt good and gave me the boost I needed to keep going. It gave me purpose when I saw myself being a helper and working for others. Even though I was dying, I decided putting others before myself was the focus. I had to find a way to make that happen repeatedly. I did and I was pretty good at it too, I truly loved helping someone in any way.

When it did happen, and every time I helped someone find the right way to come from the right place, they gave me the energy I needed to make it to the next day. Had I not made this realization, I would have been gone a long time ago, not always coming from this standpoint. God used me as one of his tools in his toolbox and used me however, whenever, and on whomever that needed help.

Do not be surprised when you get what you ask for, especially when asking God! When it does happen, I do not think you can select assignments or whom you help, and you cannot opt out because something is too hard or choose easier tasks. You help whomever God puts in front of you, the ones that need help the most at a particular time.

While God was sending some serious things my way, I did not freak out or shy away. I embraced it and felt like God was giving me a chance to do something great before it was my time to go. To do this for others that were in need and not for myself was empowering. In the moments I was in the most need, I was compelled to help others first, instead of choosing my selfishness, from which this idea of helping others was born. Evolving to this thought process was not easy and neither was keeping those thoughts at bay about when I get MINE.

I had already received much before I ever realized that. This gave me a higher purpose as God truly was using me as one of his tools from his toolbox.

At first, I was a bit overwhelmed but then one day it hit me. 'God has a lot of confidence in me to give me all this with the shape I am in currently.'

What he was giving me he knew I could handle. This gave me the shot in the arm I needed to keep preparing for this fight and enduring the wait. On towards the path to transplant, a path once thought unimaginable. I am too far away for a sick man to see with my eyes but close enough to have a vivid picture in my mind. I learned that when you help others first, you eventually get that help you need and when you help yourself first, selfishly you usually end up alone. Nobody wants to be around a selfish self-centered person, even if they are facing death.

Facing death or being ill is not an excuse to behave poorly or treat others in a harsh and nasty manner. Jesus was nailed to the cross and he was praying for those who put him there. No *Why Me or Poor me,* just asking his Father to forgive them for they knew not what they had done. Putting others before himself regardless of his own needs was a very necessary and important lesson learned for me. This is what I had to emulate, but Jesus was perfect I was far from it.

That did not mean I could not give my best effort with mistakes and my flaws and all. This powered me through each day and soon the focus on me dying was changed to focus on living to be a helper. I needed help but I needed to be a helper more. First before anything else. This is what led me to my first donation.

When I first got sick, I had really long hair, and showering became more difficult. Once the bathroom steamed up, I could not breathe. Well one day I heard about an organization that makes wigs for sick kids who lost their hair due to their treatments.

There I was getting ready to shower and I thought to myself, "I have all this hair that I cannot take care of anymore and somewhere a child does not want to leave their house because they have none." Well, it was an easy decision to make; besides, it would grow back. "If it helps make someone's life better and easier, it is the right thing to do."

I was not directly saving a life, but I was providing something that someone needed to make things easier and in an already extremely difficult situation. What you put out there comes back to you on full display and this brought me happiness. A great deal more than I expected. I shaved my head bald for the most possible length and mailed it off. I felt like I had made a difference in a world that seemed like it did not need me anymore.

I ended up doing it three times, and selfishly always hoped I would see the kid sporting my locks because that would be super awesome. I would definitely give them a compliment and then a high five, and a hug. I know it made a difference for someone, but more so, it made a difference in me.

When you are waiting for something, whatever it may be, staring at the clock and calendar only prolongs it and serves to drive you crazy.

Action, however, does make a difference and escape from the constant reminder of death hovering nearby lurking in any shadow it could find.

I guess that is why I always have to try and stay in the light so I can see the coward hiding, trying to hang around. Even though my health was compromised, I still had opportunities to facilitate goodness and do right by others before thinking of myself first.

People would ask if I were frustrated waiting and I would simply say, "NO, every day I wait I prepare myself and strengthen myself for God's perfect timing."

This all took my battle to a new level and many others joined me and made it their battle too. Without the help of family, friends and even strangers, I could never have done this on my own. I will forever be grateful for all those that helped me on this journey. Without all of you and you know who you are, the road would have been lonely and considerably shorter.

The story of my life would have ended too soon and not fully and righteously lived and that would have been a truly sad one. Waiting for anything requires patience and determination. Waiting, and only just doing that without action, is resigning to the situation because the work necessary is too hard. Yes, it is hard work dying especially when you are young.

Just the thought of an unfulfilled life is a horrible one. Sitting idly by is equivalent to quitting. They cannot win because they quit and never finish the race. We have to make sure, when we are waiting, we are not waiting for someone to die, we are waiting for the opportunity to continue and share life.

Every day twenty-two lives are lost while waiting for the call. I pray for these that never receive the gift of life and that they realized the gift their life was before it ended, and they went on to the next phase of their journey.

Are we worriers or we Warriors? Are quitters or we Conquerors? Are we Fearless or fearful? Are we Powerful or powerless? People say you only live once, but I say you only die once you have to live every day! One day at a time is all we get. Wasting any part of ourselves, opportunities, our precious resource that is our energy, only serves as self-sabotage and will always and badly.

I know it seems impossible to rebuild yourself when you are in a bad situation, sick or dying but it is not. It will be one of the hardest things you will do, no doubt, but one of the most liberating and strengthening things you can ever do.

When you can accomplish this then you will know that waiting has its purpose. Use that time wisely and purpose driven. It helped me move forward by helping others. I felt useful again and that mattered.

When you are doing for others and expecting nothing, you are working directly from the heart where we live from the most.

Being a helper empowered me in a way that helped me keep going through unimaginable circumstances and obstacles.

I pray for humility and to be able to continue being a helper. Then I ask for forgiveness from the ones I didn't bring good or positive into their lives, but the opposite, dysfunction, chaos, or worse.

Chapter 10

When God says it is Time

I remember it like it was yesterday when my phone rang, and it was the team. "Get to the hospital NOW, it is time to go!"

That is what I heard after I said hello. It was a rush to get there, but getting there safely was a challenge, the last and most important one, if this was going to happen. I could not walk anymore at this time, so my Momma would wheel me around the hospital in one of their chairs like a little white-haired Superhero. She is as tough as anybody who has ever been tough, and she kept me alive day in day out.

The first time my Dad was still with us, and they did an excellent job. I was so fortunate and blessed to have them by my side every step of the way. This time, she was alone in Phoenix with the help from my Daughter and those in my life at the time. However, she did it mostly alone before my transplant and after I was released from the hospital.

What we went through together then still helps me now, as I helped in her caregiving. She passed away in January of 2023, after a seven-year battle with Stage 4 Lung Cancer. She was seventy-seven at the time, and without her strength and faith, I would have never made it home to put my footprints in the New Mexico dirt again.

My Daughter was about twenty and she stepped up for me in a big way. In January of 2016, my daughter had some vacation time, and she wanted to spend it with her Grandma and me. She flew out at the exact perfect time on January 22.

God's perfect timing on display again, and we did not even know it. The one person I had been fighting for the whole time was on her way to me not knowing she was going to be in a front row seat for the whole thing.

I was so blessed she was because even though the severity of the situation was unimaginable, the opportunity to strengthen an already strong bond was right there and ready for us to take hold of. We sure did do exactly that. Mature way beyond her years she showed me she was more than ready. There we went after the call on our way to the hospital.

Everybody reacts differently in high-pressure situations, and the person driving me to the hospital was no different. This person being my Brother who had just got into Phoenix earlier in the afternoon with my Sister-in-law to bring my Mom her car. He was speeding and texting while driving and getting too far ahead of my Momma and the vehicle she was in behind us.

I know my Daughter was scared in the back seat and I was too and with the ride not going well, I finally told him to slow down and give me the phone. He was actually texting his kids to start praying because I got the call, so he was well intentioned. I prayed for calm mostly and for my Daughter and Brother. Well by God guiding us, we made it.

I then asked him to open the door upon arrival. Sitting there frozen staring blankly at me he rolls the window down. I was about to lose it and then some type of calm came over me and I said, "I meant the door I can not crawl out of the window." Saying it as a joke I am not sure how it went over but in the moment I really didn't care because it was funny to me.

Then comes the white-haired superhero woman, whipping around the corner pulling to the door with the wheelchair. She was on it, bringing her A-plus game. She got me out of the car and into the wheelchair all by herself and we are off to our next step.

I got there and they took me to a room immediately where two men were waiting. The last instructions were for me to shower and use a special soap.

Wait, why did he say shower?

The thing that was the worst thing for me, the one that caused the most anxiety, the times that took me closest to the edge of death. Yes, that thing. Oxygen dropping to the 60s, heart rate in the high 150s. I still do not know how I survived those. The feeling came over me for an instant that I was not going to make it and then I reminded myself that if I died in the shower, I was still fighting to make this happen. I had made it this far, it was just another hurdle to get over in the long line of them I had already crossed.

The light at the end of the tunnel was getting brighter, but mine was growing weaker as the clock ticked. The shower had already turned to anxiety and traumatic stress that still has not left me to this day.

I never take baths, and my showers are generally wrapped up in a very thorough five minutes. I just do not enjoy long showers, maybe someday it will be different, but that day has not happened yet. Every time I took one, I felt death was imminent. It was never more than a minute and a half but felt like an hour of torture that left you teetering on the edge of death every time.

The aide told me they would be right outside and if I needed them, to pull the red cord and they would come in to help me. I started washing from my neck to my waist and I was trying to hurry before everything started happening the way it always did. All of a sudden, I got weak, lost my vision and hearing, and collapsed on the chair. I could not reach for the chord and feeling like this was the end. I lunged, got it in between my fingers, and started yanking it as if I had missed my bus stop.

I know God sent those two. They told me the doctor would be in shortly and then the bigger of the two said, "You are a tough Bro, you got this. God bless you Brother."

Trying to fathom how close to death I had come in the last hour I said to myself that I had better get my shit together or this is the end of the road. Did I want to die here? I did not think so!

Then the doctor walked in and laid it all out there. I was 120 pounds with a pulmonary embolism the size of a nickel, had been bedridden for almost six months, and I was the weakest I had ever been in my life. Now what?

The doctor looked me dead in my eyes and said, "Mark, the chances are really high that you don't make it through this." I mean he was not wrong, and I had felt it going this way day after day. It was what he said after that, that let me to knowing I was in the right place.

"Even though this is reality, I promise to fight for you with everything we have available to us."

I replied, "Well Doc, I had already known the first, but now I believe the second part, and that's all I need. I am ready if you are because there's 100% chance, I won't make it if we don't get in there."

Then something came over me that I just had to let out. I had to communicate this and make sure he knew I was serious.

I told him "Doc if there is someone else with a better chance, give the lungs to them, and another thing, I don't want to be kept alive just to fully deteriorate. Take my good organs and give them to someone so they can have extra time like I had."

Shocked by the statement I had just made, he followed with this; "You know what you are saying right?" I told him I was aware, and these were my wishes because I so badly wanted others to experience what I had to receive the gift of life. And I was serious too, because then my life would really mean something.

He then told me the words I will never forget. He said, "Well that's the thing Mark, you're the only match in the 500-mile radius and we can't go beyond that. These lungs are yours no matter what. No matter what. I'm ready to fight when you are."

I said, "Well, what are we waiting for let's do this!" I asked him to call my Daughter in and what followed was the most difficult yet necessary discussion I would ever have in my entire life.

This is my Baby, my Little Special, my Everything. She was the main reason and purpose for fighting so hard to not quit and get to this day. I did not want to leave her in this world without me. I sure did not want this to be our last conversation, so I reached out to God.

I said, "God, I don't know where I'm going, or how this ends, but I know how I got here, and it's because of that little girl right there, who has grown into a woman right before my eyes and the world. Wherever you take me, God bring me back to my little girl please God."

I had to muster up the courage for the right words to make sure it did not seem like an apology or final goodbye. I had to reassure her I would be fighting to get back to her, but also let her know what I expected of her if I did not make it. I saw at last, how amazing and courageous my Daughter had been, but knew she was headed for some very scary days ahead. She knew I loved her more than anything, she knew I would fight like a true Warrior, and she knew my expectations of her going forward. God blessed me when he sent my Daughter and every day since she saved my life. She just did not know that it was the day she was born. I told her to make sure that my grandchildren knew who I was. Take them and show them my work and tell them, "You know who did that?" Your Grandpa did that." Make sure they knew who I was, but more importantly, make sure they knew who Jesus is. I then told her to call in my Mom.

My Momma came in and asked, "What do you want me to do, Son?"

"Just pray Momma, just pray." I had no idea how much further than the OR my journey would go and yeah it did go far away and then back.

Chapter 11

When will you be out of the Woods?

Someone asked me that once after transplant. They mentioned that I looked great, my skin color was good, and I appeared much stronger. Then they asked,

"When will you be out of the Woods?"

I thought about it for a second and then said, "Oh, about a week after my funeral."

See the thing about transplants is they can change at the drop of a dime. It happened to me more than once, more than a few times. Double lung transplants are the riskiest because lungs are the only organ that is not protected by the body from the outside world.

Whatever you breathe goes directly into them and that can be anything. I have gone from feeling great to being admitted from a clinic visit.

Well, I guess I'm writing about it because I'm leaving on a plane for a clinic visit and a bronchoscopy. That's where they put you under and go inside your lungs with a camera and take biopsies and look for micro bacteria. You never ever are out of the woods because there will never not be germs, viruses, bacteria, pollution and all the other crazy things that pass through our lungs.

So, why waste energy trying to get out of the woods you can't leave and put that energy into learning how to live, survive, and even thrive in those very same woods? Why not make these woods your own, and make these woods work for you instead of against you.

After the procedure they show you pictures and explain what is what, but it all looks like pink tubes or tunnels in a science fiction movie. The reason I say this is because during one bronchoscope I woke up and watched it on the big screen in the room while it was going on. I saw in my own lungs and airways. God's designs and engineering are amazing to say the least.

I woke up and could see perfectly under the cloth over my eyes and saw things I'll never forget. I saw my gift of life on the inside and those images are pressed into my memory bank deeply.

They realized I was awake watching, and they gave me some more bye-bye baby good night juice and the show was over.

I remembered when the Doctor came in, I don't know who was more amazed, me or him. At the same time, we said (him first) "What are you?" (Then me) "What was that?"

He said it again kind of jokingly "What are you man?"

I laughed and said, "The make us a little different where I'm from Doc!"

Then with my eyes wide open in amazement, I said, "It looked like tunnels from Land of the Lost. He looked at me strangely, shook his head and walked out saying the same thing again.

"What are you man?" I was lit up like a Christmas tree, so I was laughing my head off and I said, "I know what I am "A man whose has seen inside his lungs."

The one thing I learned that has helped in this transplant life is your sense of humor and ability to laugh at yourself and your struggles is what keeps you going. I mean how many people can say they have seen inside their lungs when the camera was still in there?

You must laugh and joke with the people helping you, it's good for them too. I've made more nurses laugh coming out of procedures and waking up off the anesthesia than I can count. It's some funny stuff and I'm not saying that because it's my material.

Everything from "Great party man let's do it again next weekend" to the good old "I think you guys put the wrong kind of mushrooms on that pizza, Bro!"

I've said some silly stuff in my days in recovery for sure. The all-time worst was when I went for a colonoscopy, and they asked me if I knew the man sitting next to me. I said, "Yes, he is my friend, he brought me because he had one before, so he knew I'd need help. Oh yeah, he also wants a second opinion can you help him out?"

Oh man before I realized those words came out of my mouth the nurses were cracking up uncontrollably. Heck everyone was. My buddy was mad, but at least he got me home. It was just a joke.

Truth is, it is very scary knowing they can take you from here to there and back again that quickly. There is s reason only Doctors should administer it. One of my best performances didn't come in recovery it happened in the ICU after my second double lung transplant.

I don't know why they gave me a feeding tube and not one on the other end for waste removal. I had an accident, and I felt so bad because I couldn't even say anything with the ventilator in my mouth or do anything about it. I felt so bad I was trying to apologize but it just sounded like scared gibberish mumbling.

So, the aides came and cleaned me up only for it to happen again about 30 minutes later. I knew they weren't happy, but they were professional and continued their jobs in a positive manner and that kept me from freaking all the way out having two grown men change me like a baby. It was humbling for sure but what would come next would be even more humbling.

They weren't going to have this happen again, so they sent in the Big Gun, the Real Deal, The Red Headed nurse with big forearms. A strong woman, she walked in with that 'I'm not here to screw around face and that's when she grabbed it.'

Yeah, she white knuckled that bad boy and rammed it home without even as much as a warning. Dry as the dessert sands, using both hands she slammed the rest in. No lube, no warning, no little strokes on the head telling me it only hurts a little, nothing, nada, zero.

Well at this point every hole in my body had something coming out of it except my ears, and looking back in retrospect I wish they could have filled those ones first because the things I heard still haunt me at times to this day.

I still freak out a little when I see people on the ventilator on TV, sometimes I have to step out ad gather myself.

Well eventually, I progressed, and they removed the ventilator although I was still in the ICU.

One day I'm in a mood wanting to mess with someone or crack some jokes and laugh. With God's perfect timing on display again, in walks the redheaded nurse with the big forearms.

Walking in looking strong and ready to complete her task, I said to myself, "It's Showtime baby! Breath in breath out, let's do this."

I began glaring at her with the most pissed off face I think I've ever put on and followed her with my eyes everywhere she went.

Then she finally asked me, "is something wrong?"

I said in a low voice "You're damn right something is wrong!"

She snapped back in a stern voice "Well what is it then?"

She was a tough ICU nurse who had probably seen it all and wasn't about to back down. She glared back at me with a scowl of her own.

I replied again doing my best Dirty Harry imitation "Don't think I forgot about what you did to me."

She had enough and yelled back, "What did I do to you?"

She wasn't about to be messed with and was showing that toughness that made her such a great nurse in such a high-pressure unit.

I said these words with a straight face looking down the middle of her eyes "You shoved that tube in me without even a warning, no, don't worry it only hurts at first, no stroking my hair telling me I'll be okay, no pats on the back saying be brave, it only hurts for a little while, nothing. You just rammed it home prison style with no lube!"

Her reaction was instant and obvious and as she softened up a bit she said, "I'm sorry but I had to do it quickly. I was just doing my job."

That is when I hit her with, "Well you know what you're doing when I get out of here? Before she could answer I said, "You're taking me to dinner! You can't do that to me and not buy me dinner and another thing,"

She turned and looked at me and said, "oh yeah what else?"

I replied quickly, "and I'm ordering dessert just letting you know."

I kept a straight face for as long as I could and then I just busted with the biggest belly laugh I'd had in a while because I could breathe again.

Thanks to my former acting coach Ellen Blake, when I was in my early 20s, or I would have never been able to pull it off.

We laughed so hard, then she left my room only for me to hear the nurses station erupt in laughter minutes later.

That was good medicine and healing for everyone. After four nights of not being expected to make it through to morning and nine days in a coma, there was laughter and that was another miracle.

We must always remember as we go through these hard times our smile and laugh are some of our weapons we use in the battles we face daily as Warriors.

Living this life, you just have to learn to live, survive and strive in the woods because you won't ever leave them. So, make them part of you, in your heart and soul and your mind so they never leave you or the experiences that built you as a Warrior. You'll have great days and many of them. But the second you think you're out of the woods you'll get a reminder of some kind to let you know the woods will always be right there.

It's up to us to learn to navigate and negotiate our way through this forest of transplantation and the new life we have been gifted in front of us. The thing about transplants is you don't get your old life back; you never will be there again.

A new life, new challenges, new struggles and new opportunities. You get a new life with a new component that can work for you. You get the chance to still make a difference in a new way and that is miraculous.

Even if you are fortunate enough to be able to return to some of the things you did before in your previous life as I did, you'll definitely have to figure out how to do it differently if you want to do it badly enough.

You'll have a much better appreciation for it and certainly never take it for granted again. You now have organs from another person and more time to give others what has been given to you and that's a beautiful place to be in.

Transforming from the one being helped to being the helper. God is awesome!

Chapter 12
After Beating all Odds

What do you do after you beat the odds, or the worst of odds, or when you come out on top when you weren't even given odds?

When nobody thought, you were going to make it but somehow you did. What could you possibly set up for your next move? That'll always be a tricky one to answer because I promise you everyone's answer will be different before and after you beat the odds.

Before transplant it felt like I was the only one left giving me a chance. The Doctors were very clear about my situation and others I would see looked at me as if they were doing so for the last time and for good reason.

I was in my final hours and that led to a final minute, then a second. Then I went somewhere else. My heart stopped on the table, and I experienced what can only be described as the battle for my soul, and I had a front row seat.

When I woke up out of a coma 8 days after surgery there were three things I immediately recalled. When I came out of the coma, I had the ventilator coming out of my face so I couldn't speak.

I motioned to my Daughter to bring me a pencil and paper so I could write. Well, I thought I was writing good, but when I looked at it all I could see something similar to what was on the heart monitor. I tried again with only more frustration, because all I could manage was lines which resembled what was on the monitor. All it did was increase my heart rate and in comes the nurse and I'm told to stop.

For the next 5 days I was going crazy, I so badly needed to tell somebody what I saw and experienced. After the ventilator was removed, I had these detailed descriptions of three occurrences, but as I explained to one person after another, I was told I was heavily medicated and those were hallucinations.

I was told, "You were in a coma you couldn't remember anything," but I know what I remembered, and it felt real and different.

I always found it odd and like something was being withheld from me.

Well, my questions would be answered some five months later, in an out-of-body experience, triggered by the sound the equipment makes when one's heart is shocked to start it up again.

I was not hallucinating, and a 9-day coma felt like 5 minutes. This wasn't that and I knew it and felt it in my heart, mind and soul.

I couldn't remember leaving my room, talking with several people before surgery and the prep or what the OR looked like, but I remembered these three things plain as day like they just happened minutes before.

I remembered the front row seat I had to the battle for my soul.

The first occurrence I was in a big building or house or something, but it was weird and different because it had no walls or ceilings. Somebody would call my name, and I'd look, and they'd say, "Mark I want to help you" and then they started moving towards me. First, the skin changed to like a reddish black tint, then the eyes changed, yellow on the outside and red on the inside, then the voice, the ears then eventually the horns would sprout out of their head, and I would get scared and take off running. I could see those yellow eyes with red in the middle and I could hear that voice, and I would run as hard as I ever had. This thing whatever it was transformed into a demon, I felt a fear that was unknown to me. This place was weird with no walls, no doors, no ceiling. I kept moving into different areas with the same thing happening. Well, I moved to another area and there was a countless amount of these things all coming for me. I felt cornered in a place without walls and that's when I heard this big booming voice call out and demand, "LEAVE THIS MAN ALONE, HIS SOUL BELONGS TO ME! NOW BE GONE!"

Then a huge hand gets me and moves me in the way a parent would move their child behind them if they sensed danger to shield them or protect them. This is what I felt and again the voice said, "BE GONE!" The demons turned into smoke and immediately were taken away by a strong wind.

The second one I was standing on the edge of a cliff. I looked down and I was wearing brown pants but no shoes. I wasn't wearing a shirt. And I was on my tiptoes and my momentum was pushing forward. I tried getting back on my heels, but I was unable to because of a hot wind pushing on my back. Giving it all I had I just couldn't do it and I went over the edge.

As I looked down, I could see flames, I could see red, yellow, and orange ones. Then there were the blue flames and whatever went into those burnt up fast, but the silver ones, whatever dropped in those ones was gone instantly, burned up so fast there was not even any smoke.

About halfway down I felt a humongous hand reach down and pull me back up and again place me behind as what I perceived as a place of protection. Then the booming voice says, "Do not worry my son I have you. Your soul belongs to me."

The third one I was in this huge space, completely dark, I couldn't even see my hand 10 inches in front of my face. I can't really describe the size but only to say, imagine the biggest airplane hangar ever times 1000.

Once again, no walls, no ceiling, no boundaries. Pitch black all I could see was the smallest, and I mean miniature, speck of light, way off in the distance. I saw it and was curious, so I began moving towards it.

My body then begins to raise up vertically about 25-30 feet and then smoothly turns horizontal. As I begin to move towards the light, I'm scared now and nervous. I look behind me and see a box on my back about 8-10 inches high and wide and my skin had grown over it. There were four propellers there spinning away, like smaller drones all working in unison. I get near the light finally, but I can only make out people and a bed, but not really clear. So, I flew to the front of the bed and who do I see but myself in that bed. Tubes coming out of my abdomen, lines coming out of my neck, chest, arms, ventilator out of my face, everything just as I was in the ICU with monitors and all. The sounds and lights on full display.

Then I looked behind the bed and I saw Jesus, and some of us will be surprised when we see him because the versions of him down here aren't even close. To his right he is holding hands with my Dad and to his left he is holding hands with Michelle Stella, and they are holding hands with Jamie Munoz, my first mentor and lung Donor.

Michelle was my first ANGEL HERO and Jamie who is one of my first mentors he taught me about being a recipient, he taught me about meds and side effects, he taught me about being a man of service, a helper, and a man of God.

He was my Lung Brother, and I loved him, and I am still grateful for this man and his family. They were all holding hands in a circle around me in the bed and then at the same time, the same way, they all looked at me and nodded off in the same direction. They looked back at me and motioned again with their eyes and heads in the same direction as if to say without words, "You must go now, you aren't supposed to be here. Go now." That's when I received the message that there is more work to be done.

This is when the surgical team must have got my heart jumpstarted and going again. They were right about one thing I couldn't remember anything when I was in a coma.

When I died unknowingly to me, I went somewhere for an amount of time. Probably not long but long enough for all of that to take place and it was a lot. That somewhere was a ringside seat to the most incredible and vivid images I've ever experienced.

Things so incredible I don't even know if words do it justice. As if I hovered there looking at the renewed and restored faces and bodies of my loved ones and my ANGEL HERO in awe and wonder and the sheer power that emanates from Jesus.

I kept noticing what I thought were strong grains in wood flooring planks catching my attention from the bottom of my eye. They were thick and noticeable. As I began to fly away what I thought were grains in wood planks were actually the fingerprints of God's hands and they were massive and all of us were like a tiny grains of sand in his hands.

I've never felt so protected in that moment, so loved, so blessed. They needed me to go back because the battle was far more intense than it's ever been.

I remember these three things vividly, clearly, like it was yesterday. I expressed it the best way I can but to do full justice is it really possible?

I'm not sure about that.

These are things that leave some shaken forever and others ready for any battle while fearing not one. The first people I told this to had different reactions, but all passed them off as hallucinations or something like that because of the medications. They forgot one thing though, I had done this before and these things I remembered were not hallucinations, that much I did know.

They were right I couldn't remember anything when I was in a coma, but the explanation of hallucinations just didn't feel right. My hands didn't work, neither did my legs. I had to relearn a lot of things like walking and writing.

I couldn't enunciate words properly or swallow anything. I just felt different and confused about it all. Something wasn't adding up and you know what else didn't add up.

I didn't realize till a few days after I woke up, but still had the ventilator. Racking my brain going crazy I kept thinking how they were holding hands around me like that, but they were telling me to go back to an operating table because it wasn't my time yet. I could feel their protection in that moment. They were telling me to go back to a place, from a place I hadn't been to yet, but would eventually be. They sent me back from an ICU I had not been to yet.

I know it sounds crazy, how do you think I felt, with this thing coming out of my face and couldn't even say a letter much less a word. Forget about getting a whole sentence out. My transplants were like day and night compared to each other. It's not really a thing that you are better at when you do it again after gaining experience.

The different ways I would feel after life leaving the body and there were different ways that I felt like I was leaving my body.

Before the first, it was slow and draining of energy constantly. Ups and downs, too many to count. Constant struggling but was still able to build myself stronger for the surgery.

The second time, I would feel the life leave my body quickly and very intensely. Taking me to the edge many times. Small slight movements felt like I was driving this and making it happen.

The first time I saw the black cloud of death. The second I felt my soul leaving my body. The first I was active in moving until they called me. The second I was on my deathbed for several months just fighting for the next day, the next sunset, the next hour. By living and fighting like this, I got to know God like I never had before in my life.

The first one I was down to my last days, the second I was down to my last hour. The first I was working out 2 1/2 hours a day, like an obsessed beast. Using two large tanks in this session I had it in my head that if I worked hard enough, I could get better on my own or if I died working out at least it would be in a gym kicking some ass, so I'd die happy. That's what kept me going.

The second I could not do anything except for the 11:00 o'clock hour, that was it. As soon as it hit 12, I was back to deathbed guy barely breathing. It was the strangest thing that within this hour I could breathe normally. It was the only time I could exercise and build myself for the eventual lifesaving surgery.

I had a huge pulmonary embolism and any movement I was risking death. Going to the bathroom 15 feet away was risking my life and showers were like torture to the edge of death. I would have to sit there sometimes 15 minutes just to be able to regroup and get back in bed.

I know I have some issues with PTSD from this amazing, traumatic and successful journey, and I wouldn't change anything about it. Not even a minute of it. Not even the worst minute of it.

Being aware that every time I left that bed there was a high chance I would die and not make it back was testing. But, in the end, it made me more fearless every time I did it.

Not realizing this too much later I knew that every time I did make it back it was a miracle. Even with that ticking bomb in my lung. There were miracles happening every day since the quitters in Colorado showed their true colors and I went on a mission to show them I added more than two months.

They could have treated me and that bomb inside me waiting to go off, but they quit on me, and Michelle but mostly on themselves. Losing Michelle's gift damaged me in many ways, and they didn't even care enough to try. I wasn't worthy enough to them to give their best fight, those who carried a banner for U.S. News and World Report, and they didn't know me anyway because I was just a number.

When you beat death or cheat it, however you want to look at it you can get stuck in what I call battle ready mode, and you get confused and think everything is a battle to the death.

Even the little things. It can get stuck like a dial, and you can't turn it down. That can be a positive but to be like that too long for everything will surely have negative effects. Everything is NOT a battle to the death!

It was a battle for me to not let it become that and my eventual downfall. I am not sure if I thought nothing could hurt me or more of, I wasn't afraid to go heads up and find out.

After beating the odds when you weren't given any, after beating death, and being around to talk about it makes you feel some kind of way. If you aren't grounded, have a good relationship with God or solid people around you to keep you in check and make sure your safe and healthy it could turn bad quickly and will need to be dealt with sooner rather than later.

Finding your place and purpose post-transplant is harder for some more than others but it's just as important for all. Dealing with all that transplant life brings to your day-to-day and adjusting to your new normal is never easy and that's why I love all my Transplant Brothers and Sisters and respect them so much because we have to do all this knowing the bottom will eventually fall out again and possibly be worse.

Chapter 13

Finding Your Way Without Losing Your Mind

After all that surrounds transplant finally subsides and the recovery and rehab are done, you realize they are never really done. These are not things that end. It's like they just move into a different phase or phases.

Some go back to work successfully, others not that fortunate. Some of us had jobs and careers that we couldn't return to. What I have learned from this journey of transplantation is that everything needs to be done in steps with a definite progression plan, appreciating the small victories and remembering the only constant is change.

It's extremely difficult to have plans and goals in such an unstable situation that can change at the drop of a dime. That's why I've learned small steps lead to the bigger ones and skipping steps is a for sure way to trip and fall. I've also kept in mind the importance of having one long range goal. We must always have something to work for that is a long way off it serves as a carrot to keep us moving forward and chasing something we want and need.

Not being able to do things we once did isn't always a bad thing because some of those may have led to or contributed to our downfall. There is no more rushing or being unprepared because that could lead to disaster really quick. I've learned planning and patience are my friends and they help me to not waste my most precious resource that is my energy.

Even realizing these things it's still difficult to find where we belong for some of us, in cases of people getting sick from their work can be extremely difficult.

Many times, they've spent a career doing something that has made them sick. What can they do now? How do you reinvent yourself after something like this? How do you find something that gives you that fire in your belly to be the best? How do you find something you love and want to do every day?

Honestly speaking my life was awful without stonework. I had done it for so long and truly loved my craft creating beauty from stone. I've done many things, but nothing got my fire burning like stonework did.

Well, when someone is trying to find this place of belonging or where they want to place their energy the bills keep coming in, the world keeps spinning regardless of who got sick. Figuring all of that out is our challenge, our responsibility. When you're living on extra time it's real frustrating to feel like it's being wasted when you're involved in things that don't quite give you what you want and need. I can recall times when I couldn't even land a job and they hired teenagers for, and it was a serious low point for me. Usually when these low points hit, you can be sure they can go lower if you aren't careful.

The bank is calling telling me they are coming for my Grand Cherokee. I lost my health insurance, and do you remember that growing stack of bills? Not being able to get a job with financial problems looming and growing, I had to do something that would bring money fast.

I wracked my brains for options. The money problems became too big my faith got really small and I was mad. After all the suffering and struggling I did and went through it was just to be healthy for more of it from different places?

I was wondering why God had me here and this is where the darkness began.

Was it just for more pain, suffering, and struggling on the agenda? Was it always how I worry about how I'd survive? It was taking a toll on me mentally and I had to do something fast with no good options I might add.

Why I lost faith now I can't say exactly. It had to do with losing it all again, getting sick because I couldn't afford my medicine and not feeling like I'd got anywhere even though I'd been to hell and back in my battles. Losing it all scars you in a way internally in your soul you can't fix. For me it did anyway. I was a worker, a provider, a man who made it happened with my hands. The first time I lost it all, a house, my business, all my equipment, my truck, my career, but I was still alive. I put it in my head I'd never let that happen again no matter what I had to do to never let that happen again.

Making financial decisions when you're desperate and lacking faith, well that's just a dangerous combination. You can bet on one thing for sure, it will end badly at some point. There is no doubt about that.

Well, I made a conscious decision to get involved in something that was not only risky and dangerous but plain stupid. I did so knowing the consequences full well. I saw no other way out of this problem, no possible way to get the money I needed so quickly so I made the choice. Yeah, it was a bad choice. It was my choice. My bad choice. I really can't stand it when people call their bad choices mistakes when they end badly and it's time to face the consequences of those bad choices. Let's be clear here, mistakes are when you fill out your form incorrectly or you take the wrong exit on the freeway. Those are mistakes.

Bad choices are done so willingly knowing what can happen. Why when a choice ends badly why do we attempt to call it a mistake? Why do we try and justify it by putting label on it? It's a cop out, an excuse.

I call it what it is a bad choice, my bad choice. I chose to run on the dark side knowing what was there and why I was as well. I knew deep down inside I wasn't right, but desperation and lack of faith are blinders and there I was off and running with them.

I saw no other way and I made the move. Regardless of the outcome I'll never be ashamed because it's part of my story and I'm proud of how I handled it and turned some thing ugly into something positive. Many people look for brooms and rugs or dark corners in the closet to hide their crap but not me. My Dad told me a long time ago, "You have to own your bad stuff more than you ever own your good."

He also taught me when you screw up you own it, fix it, and then learn from it as to not repeat it. He also said the measure of a man is not in his misdeeds but in what he does after that, is the true measure of a man. If you break your word or soil your name, you and only you can fix it. I was very fortunate to have my dad to teach me that and grateful I learned it. It served me well in those dark days.

Well, I've always been that one that can take the negative and turn it into a positive that was directed at me or I created it myself. This time would have to be no different.

A valuable lesson I learned at this time was that you could still spread light even though I was cruising on the dark side. I started this because I needed money for my meds and these bills and everything piling up. I quickly caught up in a very ugly game, a game that ruins lives and takes them. My anger and desperation led me to make this choice, a bad one, but mine, no doubt.

At this point, I wasn't concerned about testing fate or much of anything. I became reckless and ready for any kind of fight. Before all this sickness or anything happened, I had always been a worker from a very early age. I can recall going for loads of wood at age five with my Dad and actually working not just there to eat the lunch my Momma made us.

I started working for money at age 7 because I saw that elderly neighbors needed things done that I could do. So, I asked my Dad to hook me up with some of his old tools and started getting business. My Dad didn't just give me some old tools either, he also gave me some great words.

"Always do what you say you're going to do, never break your word," "it's either a bar of gold or a piece of crap, can't be both or change according to what you got going on," and last, but most important, "be respectful."

He was always right, and those words still have meaning in my everyday life. So, when I couldn't even land a simple job, it broke me down. Finally healthy and nobody wants me as a worker when that's all I know. I've never been too proud to do whatever I had to in taking care of my family. Now I just felt like a failure and no opportunities to turn it around. Looking back now, everything was set up for a perfect explosion that changed me forever.

I didn't know if I was mad at God or Myself for being in this situation. If I would have just protected myself all those years ago, I'd be fine now and successful and happy. If I hadn't wasted so much energy on dumb stuff, if I hadn't chosen the wrong people to be in my life, if this, if that. It was all bullshit because if my Auntie had balls, she would be my Uncle. In this world there are no "What ifs" there is only "what is". How could I be mad at God? If he saved me from death three times against all odds, so it had to be on me.

Me struggling was my fault because I never dealt with the loss of my career in a healthy and proper manner. So, I wasn't able to find happiness in other jobs or fields. It was still hanging me up. What shocked me was how easy it was for me to do things and how skilled I was at something I had never done before. I had a lot of the tricks down and also had the whole character down. I had the whole violence down thing too as I quickly earned the reputation for not being worried about taking it to the streets. I began a transformation to intolerance and inflicting whatever necessary on whoever crossed me with money. I found myself doing things unimaginable before.

I justified it all by saying I'm doing it to stay alive and get these meds. Eventually I got my insurance back, but I was caught up by now and I chose not to stop. I was caught up in the worship. I'm drowning in a sea of fakes around me. They were only there because of what I had in my pocket. The ugly game I chose was selling high-grade cocaine to people who had been drinking or drinking in the bars. I was fooling myself as if I had clout and some standing, but I was only ruining my life and possibly others. I was ruining lives and claiming my own.

I thought I had power only to find myself powerless when the House of Cards fell. Selling high grade to a bunch of party animals was definitely a way to alleviate my problem, but it only created more. I was stuck and needed help, and it wasn't coming from anyone around me. In a bad place worse than any other I have ever been in before. This time was different though because I put myself here knowingly and the walls were creeping in slowly at first and then extremely fast at the end.

I wasn't doing all bad when I was walking the dark side, so I knew I hadn't totally lost myself. Well, God sent that help in the form of drunk loud mouth looking for freebies for him and his other drunk loudmouthed friend. As I was leaving the bar I saw someone I had been avoiding the whole night. I walked by like I hadn't seen him, but he saw me and made a b-line for me.

He was waiting on me, he was drunk, broke, and wanting freebies. When I said no and started walking away, He let the wrong garbage come out of his mouth and he promptly ended up getting slammed into the ground.

After I put him on his back, I turned around to walk away only to see a police officer pulling up. He saw me do it, so he asked what was going on. I told him the drunk guy was harassing me, the drunk guy told him I had coke, and he went home, and I went to jail. A place a transplant recipient should never be. Mostly because there are a lot of people, a lot of germs, and a lot of who knows what floating in the air. I put myself here with my choices so if I got sick this could be a life sentence and the full weight of that was on me.

Knowing this, I had some time to figure out a plan for a comeback from this. I had made some big ones already, but if I was going to make this one, I'd have to make some changes in my life or I'd be another sad story that would break many hearts.

As I lay there on that concrete bed I had some great conversations with God. Only one was speaking, the one who needed to get to work on fixing a whole lot of broken. It was in that home that I Gave my life to Jesus and I heard those chains hit the jailhouse floor. It had been some time since I made legitimate money and being so disgusted in myself, I went out and found the first job I could. I was working for a handyman. Doing landscaping, maintenance, moving furniture, and any other odd jobs people needed. It wasn't the work I wanted to do, and it wasn't sufficient money to pay the bills, but it was legitimate and that's what mattered. Being physical again took some time to get used to but that wasn't the worst part of it. The worst part was everybody always asking, "Are you all right?"

I didn't want to be handled with kid gloves or have people feeling sorry for me, so I tried to outwork everyone. If something was wrong with me then they should have no problem keeping up. I work hard, I always do always have. You'd be hard pressed to find out otherwise.

One Saturday afternoon, I was having some burgers at the house with my Bro Rico, and we were talking about life, my situation, my job, probation, and everything in between.

Being that it was August 2020 and COVID was raging pretty hard, we hadn't really seen each other much because of that so it was great just to sit and talk with a great Bro.

I mentioned if I could just do stonework again everything would be OK, he then replied, "Why can't you?"

I told him I wasn't sure I could do it anymore and was basically doubting myself. He started laughing and called me out right to my face, "You are the one always saying you have to believe and now what? You say, don't doubt yourself, too many people will doubt you in your life so never become one of them. Was that all Bullshit? Do you even live by this stuff?"

He got into me pretty good, and I know why. I was feeling sorry for myself, and he gave me what a good brother would give. A bit of a mental ass-kicking and I had it coming, and I loved him for that.

He said I'd have to try and if I really couldn't then I better figure it out because what he was looking at wasn't working.

He wasn't wrong or out of line for telling me like he did, either. See the world I live in if you can't give the ones you say you love that tough love, we all need sometimes then you don't really love them. If the storm is on their heads and you make distance between your shoes and theirs, well, when the sun is shining on them again, then keep the same distance.

He believed this as much as I did, and I loved my Bro for that. He cared enough to give me the tough love I needed and, in many ways, wanted. That kick in the ass got me going.

The next Monday at work with the boss and coworker being crybabies and also not backing me up when some old, extremely racist lady pulled some extremely disrespectful crap on me I realized I was in the wrong place.

Doing the same job, I had when I was seven, and not happy doing it, I had to go so I did. I had to go to phoenix for a clinical visit the second week of August. It was a few days after I had burgers with Rico.

In Phoenix, I got a call from Rico, and we talked about how nice it was, and I thanked him for being real with me. He said he wanted to come by Thursday night and he would bring some steaks.

I told him "I'm in Phoenix Bro for a checkup, I'll be back this weekend let's do it Sunday."

He said "OK", so we planned for Sunday night steaks.

Well, it never happened because that Thursday night he wanted to come by but I was in Phoenix and he lost his life in a motorcycle accident. When I got the news, I was floored. I had just talked to him. We had plans, and now the person I wish could have been my little brother was gone. That's why I was saying I loved him because he is in heaven now.

It was in that moment that I decided to become a Stonemason again and that is how I honor Enrique "Rico" Roybal. I vowed that I would not let that conversation go in vain and that was how 'The Lung Transplant Stonemason' was born.

With no job to go to and no tools to even do stonework I had to figure it out. So, I took the money I made from my former job and made it useful for something.

I set myself up with all the basic things I'd need to start doing stonework again, and all I needed now was a job. So, I started manifesting an opportunity and voicing these words out loud, "It's going to be great chiseling stone again at my new job." Then it wasn't even a couple of days, and I had a job.

The phone rings out of the blue and there it is. Two days after that call I was on site doing stonework again full time. It was a hard first day. It was a hard first 5 minutes. I managed to smash my pinky between two rocks, busting it down to the white meat, then missed the chisel and blasted my hand with the hammer.

I looked down at my left hand already bleeding in two places, my right hand busted open, and I just started laughing.

I looked up at the sky and said, "I see what you're doing God, and I really do want to be here." Then I laughed again only to look over to see my two non-English-speaking coworkers looking at me like I was loco en la cabeza.

I made a vow that Rico's words wouldn't be in vain, and they have remained a great motivator for me. I'll never forget my Bro Rico for always being true and to this day he is the only person in my life who didn't have to say sorry to me for anything or me to him.

He was an old soul, and a great man lost too soon. I think about him all the time because he was impactful in my life and I'm forever grateful. Self-doubt is a dream killer and will keep you in a box you can't get out of until that behavior is changed.

As transplant recipients we all have to get used to and adapt to change. It starts from the very beginning with the meds. Constantly changing doses for a while to get the right levels in the blood. Adapting to a new life we have been blessed with has its challenges.

Going back and doing the same things the same way as you did in your previous life almost never works. You aren't the same person so even attempting the same activities must be done in a different manner.

I was very fortunate to be able to go backwards to find myself again many aren't. Finding my true self again on that rock pile was huge but I don't recommend going back to what almost killed you to do so. It worked for me, but a lot of crazy things work for me that should come with disclaimers.

I was so lost that it was like I wouldn't be able to move forward till I had undone some things and started to redo them again. It felt as if I had to return to that rock pile and reclaim my power and strength.

I know it sounds bizarre, but it was like I was trapped in a game of solitaire, and I had to undo a bunch of things and then do it right. That's what the healing part of all this felt like too.

In doing so, opening a bunch of wounds and checking for infection and closing it properly allows the healing to begin. That's how my rock pile and jobs were. My healing days.

I was tired of failed attempts, working for the wrong people, wrong places, settling for any job. Not knowing what was next so I decided to go back to my love and passion for stonework.

It was one of the best decisions I've ever made, and I jumped headfirst into the pool but I forgot about something. Sometimes you dive into the shallow end.

Yeah, you guessed it. Boom! The first day back hurt very bad and after the first week, I was in bad shape, but nothing compared to the pain I felt laying in that jail cell. Nothing even close.

Knowing how many people I let down that believed in me, I know what I had done and what the fallout would be. I was aware of all of that and those were the people that were driving me when I was tired, hurting, and in pain, to keep going and turn this thing around to something good and positive. A product of our love and faith in God.

Even though I lost faith, God never lost faith in me and never stopped loving me. I don't deserve it, but he gives it to me unconditionally. I am unworthy but I can keep working to be the man God knows I can be and the one he wants me to be. The man my family needs me to be.

We all have choices, I made mine and I'm ok with it. I stood up like a man and handled it appropriately. I honestly believe that I've been able to help others who have gone through similar problems. We all mess up but the ones who choose to stay messed up break my heart because they don't have to.

God is only one conversation away, but you have to give it all to Him and change what is destroying you no matter how hard it is if a good life is what you really want. A bunch of talk won't get it done only a bunch of hard work on yourself. It's possible I know. I did it.

I did some good things on the dark side too. I fed a lot of homeless people, helped a lot of people who needed money, saved two people from committing suicide, and helped three people get to rehab. None of that lessens the sting of the hearts I broke, and I'll forever be trying to mend those. None of that justifies my behavior but answering for my sins and changing my life served to show I'm genuinely in this.

So, the king of comebacks was on the road to redemption. I learned a very valuable lesson while navigating this road. This road is full of bumps, potholes, and obstacles. If you try and change your course there are no guarantees.

Traveling this road is best done alone. Only you and God. If it's something you truly want, you will figure out how to negotiate and navigate this road no matter how hard it can be.

To think about roads of redemption or recovery they are very similar. The road is super bumpy and unpredictable. You never really know what's around the next corner or curve.

Depending on how you approach it you could be setting yourself up for your greatest comeback or your next setback.

Life alters either way because there is nothing that doesn't get altered on this road. Killing your body is tough, no doubt, but healing of the soul is harder because as humans we tend to beat ourselves up unnecessarily and more so when we fail or make horrendously bad choices.

The most important thing I learned is just because the road is tough and bumpy and full of challenges it doesn't mean that that we can't take the opportunity to make it a beautiful ride and one we will never forget.

This is why I'm not ashamed and embarrassed about this part of my life. I proved to myself most importantly that with the right frame of mind and unwavering faith comebacks are always possible regardless of our own fears and doubts.

As we learn to turn down the volume on them, we are able to see more and more opportunity including the one to right our wrongs against others and ourselves.

I'm not going to lie, it's one of the hardest things I've ever done, but also one of the most empowering and fulfilling. My pain and lack of faith led me to the darkness, but God never forgot about me and Jesus walked by my side as I was putting footprints in the wrong places, protecting me. I didn't deserve that so now I live my life to repay that debt.

God never gave up on me and gave me the opportunities to help people even in that environment. Although the road is rough, we can't forget how easy it is to lose sight of what is best for us. Sometimes that means having to do the very hardest thing on the list of options. Most of the time that's the right one.

We have that choice to become stronger or allow ourselves to become weaker, but that's ours.

The road is also how we make it. We don't have to accept anything because we can control how we move our way down it. The things I take away from my days on the dark side are many and useful now. They served to not let me go back to those dark days when I lost myself and I have kept my faith strong no matter what comes my way. I know I made bad choices. I also know I didn't run and hide. I faced it like a man. I owned it fixed it, and learned from it just like my Father taught me. I also put in a lot of work to fix my name and my word. I was the only one that could do that.

These days serve as reminders of what can happen when we lose faith but also what can take place when it is restored and what we can overcome strengthening it once again. With this behind me I realized how fortunate I was to have a chance to get to be a helper and inspiring others. One of my greatest accomplishments is that I was able to get myself out of that pile of disgust I put myself in and turn all that into something positive. That's twice the power when we do that.

I know there will always be people who will talk bad about me and bring up my past. Stuff like that will never go away so here it goes.

News alert to the peanut gallery: "Go ahead! I don't live there anymore! I had the courage to change! Throwing dirt on my name, that's fine. You can think you've buried me, but all you've done is cover a seed that I watered and it sprouted, grew, and blossomed into the unheard of. The broken road and its darkness led me back to my craft. I am one in eight billion and the only one in history."

This only took place because of hard work, perseverance, discipline, a no-quit attitude and boatloads of courage. To grow from things like this is empowering and enlightening.

What I gained was far greater than what I lost. What I lost I will never forget because if I do, I'll be setting myself up for next fall. I might not get back up from that one.

Setbacks happen easy and quick, comebacks require much time, dedication, self-discipline, hard work, and an unwavering want to do good again.

I can't lie, all those people talking bad about me was a motivator and also an indicator of who belongs in my life or not. After I got in trouble, I became invisible to all the fakes and that was OK they actually did me a huge favor. I'm so fine with that.

I got myself in this mess and only I could get myself out and I knew that. Just remember when people show you their true colors, believe them and if they cut and run when the storm is on you, make sure they aren't near you when the sun is shining on you again. You can't be around for my success if you left me in my struggles.

I've forgiven and asked for it and I've moved on for my own Peace of Mind and for peace in my heart. I let go of all that negative weighing me down. Nobody is worth draining your precious energy resources and sometimes you have to go through the toughest places to find yourself and your peace again.

To do the hard work you'll be better off for it and sometimes healing means ripping the wound open and making sure all the infection is out. You have to do this for yourself. Making sure to properly heal.

It is your wound, isn't it? All you need is God and some courage to heal. Sometimes it's part of you for a while until you reach a certain point. When you reach that point and the sun is shining on you again, look around. Those were the true ones that are still standing.

I experienced many things that left me with questions about my Donor that I don't know. I truly feel like this part of my life mimicked his in many ways and this had to take place. I felt like my donor did things in his life that required that trip down the road to redemption and I felt like he was truly with me while I was on mine. In the end he did the greatest thing ever by giving the gift of life as his last act on earth.

Chapter 14

Doing the Unheard of

We've all heard about people doing things never been done and it's always amazing.

When you hear about the unheard of, it makes you wonder how this is possible?

Have you ever heard of someone going back to the dangerous life threatening and extremely labor-intensive job that did its best to try and kill that person?

Have you ever heard of someone having the most major of obstacles in their way, only to make it work for them in their favor?

Have you ever heard about the one in 8 billion guy?

The stonemason with two double lung transplants.

Hi, my name is Mark Rodriguez and I'm the 55-year-old man doing this stuff.

I guess sometimes it happens, but the first ever, that's the crazy part.

I learned the hard way not to be asking why a long time ago. I know that God didn't put me here just to do

Just B.R.E.A.T.H.E. & Believe

more jobs and limp off into the sunset. I know that for sure. So, I'm using this position to show others that we all have an unheard of and we can all tell it loud and clear.

I want to be clear here that whatever I'm using to do this you all have the same thing, I'm not different. We are all capable of doing whatever it is we want, we can all overcome, we can all overachieve, and we can all believe.

It's not just about believing though, we have to know we are good enough, first off stop with the negative self-talk and negative self-perceptions. We as humans beat ourselves up so unnecessarily.

Life is hard and confusing most days so why do we want to make it worse by punching ourselves mentally or verbally? I know without the right approach and God, I don't have a snowball's chance in the place the devil lives, of surviving. I don't!

I think there are enough people talking badly about me, so I really don't want to be like them. So, I do my absolute best to stay away from that self-sabotage. I know God doesn't like hearing that. How can I ask God to strengthen me and turn me around and beat myself up?

Even when the stonework starts to hurt and my body feels like I can't do it anymore, I know there is more because I stay away from the bad words I can't, if, but, and maybe. Why those ones? If used too much, they will weaken you and break you down to a pile of nothing.

The power in our words can drive us to new heights or show us our all-time lows. I know that with faith in our Heavenly Father and belief in yourself anything is possible. Even the unheard of.

Sometimes I let people see me work for a few days before I tell them about my story, so it blows their mind a little more. Then I say, "God is great all the time!"

At times in life, you may be the only one who believes you can do it, but that's the voice that matters the most.

I learned that asking why and how only serves to prevent me from reaching that place that was born in my visions.

I don't say, "why me?" I say, "why not me?"

Believing that God knows who his strongest soldiers are, it is hard, but if you have the confidence and skill set to make a difference then you'll understand you are being given what you can handle.

So, if it's super hard just know that God has a lot of confidence in you and believes you can do this. So, you better start having confidence in yourself and believe that you can do it as well. To give you that much is a blessing.

We get overwhelmed and depressed when we let these types of things get in the way. Going the wrong way only delays and deters us and takes our time. Time we don't have to waste.

I'm blessed that I get to wake up and thank God for opening my eyes and go do something that brings me great happiness and joy. Something that nobody else is doing like I am. I might be the only one doing this or I might be paving the roadway for the next guy.

Either way I'm making history and being a helper by inspiring others along the way. Sure, there are thousands of stonemasons better than me but not any with a lung transplant.

People ask, why I do this, and all I say is, "if you aren't doing what you love are you really living or just existing?"

If you want something, make a plan and attack it, one step at a time with determination and discipline. Before you do any of that though, you must first believe in yourself and that you are capable of doing whatever it is you placed before you.

The mind moves in thought, spoken words enter the universe and the body will always follow loyally.

Many believe we really have no idea how far it can take us. I didn't. I never imagined me being able to put years into a comeback and in one of the hardest professions there is. God did. God surely did.

It can also be dangerous if you start thinking you can do anything and can't be defeated. It requires great humility when beating the odds and doing the unheard of because once you are no longer grounded it's easy to float away and crash.

I've used my experience to help others find their unheard of and plan to be able to tell it. A lot of being a transplant recipient is knowing you're a helper because you've been helped and it's good to know there are countless ways one can be a helper.

With all the ups and downs that take place in this life you feel like a yo-yo or you're in the middle of some weird mind game. It's difficult to keep it together but that is what we are charged with so that is what we do. I have so much love and respect for my Transparent Brothers and Sisters because of this.

Unheard of, this happens all the time, and I don't think I'm something special, but I have been called to this very unique place. These types of unheard-of acts and miracles happen all the time but only when one truly believes it is possible and that we are possible and be willing to put in the work to make it possible.

By the way, this doesn't just go for transplant recipients either. Everyone should believe they are the best or how can the best come to them and into their lives?

Even if you're the only one who thinks this in the world, you're the only one that matters!

The power of positive thinking and belief in yourself can put you in a place you never thought possible. Places nobody ever gave you a chance to get to, and to do all you desire.

You can make a daunting task seem small and completed easily. It's said when choosing this the sky is the limit. Believe it to be, and it'll never be able to be measured or compared.

Every day we are given, we have a choice to be more or less of ourselves than the day before. Even when you're feeling stuck you still have choices. Stay stuck or break the hell out of that place, however you have to, in order to get to the place, you deserve to be.

Sometimes doing what is hard is the best option, doing what you don't want to do. Some have said that discipline is merely doing the things you hate to do but doing them like you love them.

Being sick isn't always the worst thing. The flip side of it is that we find our real true strengths and with our weaknesses we show ourselves our own true colors.

In tough situations everyone does, but when you show yourself, you are definitely showing your true colors to everyone. In times of sickness both our strengths and weaknesses take on their own unique glare. I guess that depends on the individual. I found out mine early on and mine were always those of a warrior.

I've learned that knocking myself for my weaknesses serves no purpose and is only a waste of time and energy. Do your best to turn them into strengths, but we all have them. If you can do that, it is a key in achieving success as the underdog or in the fight for your life.

When people say I can't, I lose it. Listen, we take what we can from others and combine it with what we bring to the table, and we go for it. When it comes to I can't, the only thing I've ever seen with my Transplant Brothers and Sisters is they can't quit. Even in the worst of times they have thrived and fought. The ones that aren't here anymore, while they won their war as the ultimate Warriors, they were awarded with a trip back home to rejoice with our Heavenly Father in God's Kingdom. This is what I believe.

I don't like it when I read in the obituaries that someone lost their battle to whatever they were up against. They didn't lose anything! They fought like worthy Warriors and were awarded the chance to go home where we all want to go someday. So how could that be a loss?

When attempting the unheard of you'll hear a lot of advice from someone who has never walked in your shoes, so just take what's helpful and useful and all the other stuff just drown it out. You have to because you need everything to listen to your own gut and mind and God.

Maybe the unheard of only exists in the minds of those who are not willing to take their shot and missed their opportunity because they didn't believe it. The unheard of only happens when someone does something everyone told them was impossible. That person never stopped believing in themselves, in their dream.

I always wonder when someone says, "you can't do it." Is it because they don't think they can, so they try and convince you it's not possible for you?

Why not put that kind of effort into crushing your fears and doubts? I always say, 'the only time we lose is when we quit, give up on ourselves, or feel sorry for ourselves.'

When we keep fighting with the belief that we are a worthy Warrior then there is no fight too big, too intense, too risky or requiring too much effort. Warriors might die, but it's always fighting and never quitting because when we do that, we are no longer Warriors. Leave this world a Warrior and arrive at your next stop a Warrior just the same.

Since this journey started, I've always been one to believe that however I leave this earth will be the way I show up to the next phase of the journey. Nobody wants to show up anywhere as a quitter, well, not any warrior I know.

Fighting day-to-day, knowing you're dying takes great faith and self-discipline. The faith, because when you get that bad like I was, like deathbed bad, God is the only one that can help.

Self-discipline comes in when you're feeling like garbage and it's time to fight. When you want to rest, but you don't want to quit. When your tank is empty but someone around looks at you with eyes that are practically screaming to you, please don't leave me and they don't even know it.

At the end, I wasn't even fighting for myself anymore. I was fighting for everyone around me, for Mari, and my Mom, more than anyone. It turns out for my Grandson as well. I didn't know that at the time.

Those two alone were worth all the pain, heartache and then some. They made my life so good. Then my wife came along, and she has been one of the biggest blessings of my life.

I was even fighting for people I didn't know yet. In these situations, that's what needs to be done. I wish I could just sit and write about all of the Warriors that absolutely blow my mind and inspire me, motivate me, and force me to ask myself, "What's your excuse today?"

Sometimes the unheard of is fighting while dying because the two really don't mix. I want to normalize the unheard of, because we believe so much in ourselves. I draw strength from what my Warrior Brothers and Sisters do, and I do what I can, always, to give them something back of value. I get it from so many sources. I do everything I can to give it back and that is how we keep going.

The unheard of is empowering, but when you help someone else find theirs, tell their unheard of story, loud and clear, that's when I feel the best. Finding your voice and purpose in this transplant life is still very important.

Helping others find theirs is where the real power and love are. It's like watching the bloom of a rare orchid, or rose, or some other beautiful work of nature. The growth that takes place is what strikes me as the most beautiful part. because that takes some real work to get there. Real hard work, and when it pays off it's truly beautiful.

Fighting day-to-day knowing you're dying takes great faith and discipline and sometimes that *is* the unheard of. I just want to normalize the unheard of.

There are Warriors out there that absolutely blow my mind and give me inspiration that allows me to draw strength from. I'm fortunate enough to get it from many sources, so I do my best to provide it for others as much as possible.

Doing the unheard of, or never done before, is empowering but not as much as helping others find theirs and tell it loud and clear. When they realize what they are capable of being, doing the unheard of is the most powerful. And therein lies an opportunity for growth. In this life of transplantation, we all learn so much about ourselves through our struggles and sacrifice.

We all do it differently, some do it publicly, others never say a word. From one end of the spectrum to the other we all have our own way of dealing with it and coping.

The ones that deal with it publicly sometimes are misunderstood as attention seekers. I do not agree with this. Can you imagine fighting so hard for something only to be told it's not working? Or when someone gives you an expiration date in your life?

I pray that everyone has a healthy outlet and strong people are surrounding them. However, that you deal with it, do it in a way that doesn't further weaken you.

Have you ever woken up feeling great and then two hours later you feel like you can't take another step? Well, some days that's transplant life, some days you feel like Superman or Supergirl, and other days you can't get out of bed because it feels like you got hit by a very large truck.

As I said before, this life isn't for the weak or faint of heart. Judging someone because of the way they choose to deal with their life and situation is just plain wrong, especially if you are a fellow recipient. Judging anybody, anytime, for anything is never a good look. Just like we are all different, so are all cases. We as humans have our own unique way of dealing with life, so who is anybody to judge another and how do they do it?

I deal with mine by being grateful because according to my doctors I shouldn't have made it. I'm grateful this team didn't quit on me and fought for me and with me.

Thank you, St., Joe's, I love you all. So, if I'm struggling or in pain where things get super heavy on my mind and soul, I say thank you to God, my Heavenly Father, because medically speaking I shouldn't even be here to feel and experience these things.

Early on in my comeback to my stonework career I was in so much pain throughout my entire body. Driving home, no music, sitting in silence, feeling the wind hitting the tears rolling down my cheeks. wondering how I'd be able to do it all over again tomorrow if God woke me up again the next morning.

One Friday after work in the shower, I was crying really hard because I was in so much pain. Little secret, I cry in the shower sometimes when I'm playing music on my phone and that way nobody can hear me.

Admittedly feeling sorry for myself a bit, all the emotion was pouring out in its worst form and then all of the sudden it stopped. My voice in my head said, "How dare you do this, you punk? You shouldn't even be here to feel this pain! You need to find a way to be grateful for this pain, you should be a worm buffet right about now!"

I thought about all my Lung Brothers and Sisters that had gone on to the next phase of their journeys after fighting as worthy Warriors. I thought about their lives and dreams and then my own. I thought about the lunches and holidays that they missed, that I hadn't, but mostly I thought about their Warrior spirits. I wondered what they would say if they saw me now.

I also thought about my Lung Brothers and Sisters in the middle of their fights, if they saw me like this, how it would affect them?

So, I said these words as the water ran down my body to the drain.

"God help me turn my pain into power, and my heartaches into helpfulness, and my traumas into triumphs."

After voicing this and giving it life into the universe, I felt the pain and suffering going away, flow down the drain as the water did and it was quite empowering. I had found the words that matched what I was feeling inside.

I kept this in my prayers, and I am still shocked by the power of these words. It's led me to a better understanding of the power of our words. How it can be crushing and defeating, or uplifting, empowering, and enlightening.

They can drive us to do great things or keep us imprisoned in the walls we've built with stones made of fear and doubt. It can be life changing or life ending. The thought becomes the word, becomes the action. First you think it, second you speak it, third the body follows orders as it always does. It works both negatively and positively.

I have found being aware of this always is extremely beneficial. We all know somebody that says I'm so dumb or I'm worthless. The ones that beat themselves up with that negative perceptions and self-talk.

Whether they know it or not they are defeating themselves with their own words and beliefs.

Being that there is a flip side to everything, the possibilities are still there even in the worst of situations. So, the flip side is positivity and belief in God and yourself.

If you have got those two working for you, then you'll be looking up quickly and seeing those very possibilities and opportunities. Go the other way with it and you can be assured the decline will be rapid, harsh, and most times unbearable.

God makes us up of three parts the body, mind, and soul. The stronger the parts, the stronger the whole.

Everybody should embrace these, not just recipients or people with major medical issues. See, as difficult and impossible as it all seems, we must always stand as courageous Warriors with our ten toes down, digging in, not backing up, or shying away from the fight.

The thing about fear is that it can be controlling, defeating and demoralizing if it's allowed to become too big. It is said that courage is not the absence of fear, it is simply the mastery of it. This could not be truer. Let's not get started on fear of the unknown.

When people are sick or hurt it's pretty easy to start the 'what if' game, or the 'what about this or that' game. I always say that somewhere out there right now, a bridge is on fire, but I certainly won't be thinking about it unless I am about to cross it. Your mind can run you ragged playing this game. It's a huge responsibility to not fall victim to your fears and doubts. We have enough battles to put our energy into. Choosing to waste it on things that don't move us forward will not make us stronger and should never be an option. Sometimes sadly it is.

We can't continue to feed our fears and doubts and then when our lives are beyond control, we start asking why. Can you imagine being the architect and builder of your own demise? Well, it happens every day and it also stops every day when one decides to believe in themselves. When no one else does!

When they are giving no odds, when you fail, the storm is on your head and you are all alone, you take that stand. Plant your feet and fight for what it is you want. Let nothing chase you from your fights or deter you from the place you belong.

Finding the flip side in an unimaginable situation is difficult but it is possible. Whether things go wrong or fall apart the easy way to go is toward the darkness, and it's way harder to stay in the light but all of the more necessary.

Being sick and expressing life's difficulties negatively or without optimism can put you in situations you never could imagine. This really makes things worse so give all that to God. He knows what to do with it better than we do.

Keeping your mind in the right place makes all the difference in your situation. Mental health takes a hit when our physical body is in bad shape or facing death. Keeping it clear and clean is best done with this strong relationship with our Creator because only our Creator can fully understand all our struggles and battles.

When you think you cannot anymore God knows you can. When you start believing in you, your faith in God become stronger as well. When we can't even love ourselves, God still loves us. We don't deserve his mercy and grace, but we get it anyway. That is why when I'm hurting on one of those truck days and it's unbearable, I think about the pain Jesus went through on the cross for all of us and then I realize my pain will never be equivalent to what Jesus went through for US and then I work on turning it into my power.

Chapter 15

Gratitude

When I first was diagnosed, I felt like the whole world was crashing down on my head all at once. Of course, I was questioning things and why this was happening. In the midst of the loss of my career, in a badly failing marriage, I was now facing death, with my daughter on the ringside seat with a close-up of it all. I had to figure something out in the middle of a depression and feeling like a caged animal. I had to figure out a way to do this.

When it feels like it is all coming down on your head, trying to find the positive or something to be grateful for is difficult to say the least. The thing about it is, when we are in the course of our daily lives, we forget about a lot of life and all of its important parts. We are wrapped up in in the day-to-day, and we lose sight of so many things we never should.

How was I supposed to be grateful to be alive after losing so much and on the verge of losing my life?

If I was not grateful for the good things and took so much for granted, how could I be grateful for silicosis fibrosis? How could I be grateful for still being alive? It had taken so much already, but would I let it take everything from me, including my last breath?

When your health declines, doctors' offices and hospitals become the norm, and you tend to see others in similar predicaments more often. This is where my opportunity to realize I had done it all wrong came with another chance to make it right and figure out this thing called gratitude.

What did I have to be grateful for though? Turns out, I had tons to be grateful for. I was just clouded by being wrapped up in the day-to-day stresses and my negative reactions to them.

If I could figure this out, this would go a long way towards changing my mindset about everything that has taken place over the course of my life. Up until now, I had to fight and work my ass off for all I had achieved.

Nothing was ever given to me, nothing but an opportunity, and it was being offered once again with a slightly different look. In the past, I worked hard at jobs, on teams, and school proving myself at every stop took all I had. I was more than willing to give some more. Now I had to be ready to give it all in the fight for my life. What should I be grateful for? Getting stuck on being the *why me* guy will definitely keep you from finding what it is to be grateful for. With so much loss, I will not lie; it was difficult to find something, anything, to be grateful for sitting in a doctor's office.

One morning it happened. I happened to sit next to someone who had definitely figured this out. I was in my early forties and people's reactions to seeing me on oxygen were all over the place. Some thought I had a disease, other thought I had smoked my lungs away, but this particular morning, I sat next to a woman who was already on the road I was about to get onto.

As I sat down, she said, hello, and I said Hi. Being in a pulmonologist's office with an oxygen tank, she put one and one together, just came out, and said it.

"Are you on a transplant list?" I replied, "No, I am not."

Her directness rather threw me for a loop, so with a bit of an attitude, I said, "Why would you ask me that?"

She looked at me and said, "I want you to know even though you are weakened, you have what you need to do this."

I was speechless and why was this woman talking to me so open and freely? She could tell by the look on my face that I was overwhelmed by it all and she looked at me and told me, "Even though I'm here with these medical issues, I know there's someone out there who would trade places with me in a heartbeat because their situations are way worse than mine."

That is why I try to help when I can to show my gratitude for still having a chance to do something positive and helpful, even though my life has many challenges.

Every morning, I wake up, I know God has given me another chance to reach out and help, and I am so grateful for everything that happened.

She then said this, "Had I never became ill, sadly, none of this would have come into my life."

I sat there speechless thinking about this woman's words. Looking back at it, I know she was sent to me to show me this lesson. Her words have been part of my thinking ever since. There would have been so many people I would not have known, or love, had I not felt ill, so many lessons I would have missed, so much growth I would not have experienced. So many lives I never would have had an opportunity to do the same thing that others did for me when I was facing my mortality, the loss of my career, and an uncertain future.

I did not know where the road I was on would take me, but now I knew for sure how I would travel it and that would make a huge difference. Since those early days on this journey, I have come to see that my hardest days are the ones I am most grateful for. Those are the ones that built me at my core and soul. When opening your eyes in the morning causes the gratitude to come pouring out of your heart, it means you are doing something right.

When a disease is rearing its ugly head, it is easy to be mad, quit, or feel like life is not fair. Nobody ever said it would be, but in our toughest moments, we still have an opportunity to spread and receive light and give others hope and inspiration. Even being so close to the edge of death, sometimes it's those days that power us to the next, the ones where we have the courage to acknowledge that others have it way worse and that we still have a chance in these moments for positivity and greatness. Even though we are close to death and knowing that there are others closer than we, this is when we have an opportunity for greatness by choosing the way of The Warrior.

Truth is, we all get closer to death every day we live, but when we are facing it head on is when we have an opportunity to live it the way God intended us to. This was the case for me. Finding gratitude. In my toughest days and moments, I turned something within myself. I never knew I had the ability to lead and help others which in turn helped me.

Helping when you are in need, leading when you have no clue where the road is going, are those things that help you get to the next day, not questioning whether or not you can do it. Whenever something happens that is difficult, I always remind myself that this is not my worst day and I got through that one, so I am going to be all right and I am going to get through this one.

It was at this time that I fully realized that worry and stress are a choice, and prayers are the best medicine and that is what can make a difference. It does not say in the Bible that worry and stress are helpful. Not even once. Worrying and stressing will never change the situation, but they will break you down from a health standpoint quickly, and if you are already sick, that is not too good, is it? Stress kills. That is a fact, but stress is a choice.

It is also a huge waste of your precious energy as well. I have learned to be grateful for my pain, being that medically speaking, I should not even be here to feel it. I ask God to help me turn my pain into power, my heartaches and helpfulness and my traumas into triumphs, and this has my gratitude at an all-time high.

People often tell me they feel bad for me because of all I have been through and to those people, I always have the same response.

"Don't feel bad for me. This is the best thing that has ever happened to me."

They look at me like I'm crazy and maybe I am, but I see what life is about and I've been able to change those things about me that had me lost living my life in a way that was not beneficial for me, my growth, and for those around me.

Drowning myself at work to avoid problems. Taking so much for granted because I thought I was in control and generally missing a lot of the good and beautiful things about life. I had to come to the edge of death to make these realizations. My growth as a man and being able to evolve in this time were great accomplishments for me, and ironically, I never felt so alive than when I was dying because I was finally doing the things that really mattered.

Looking back, I could see all my mistakes and where I went wrong, but looking forward, I was armed with a new way and a new outlook. I set out to show anyone I could that being grateful in the hardest moments of our lives brings power and opportunity to share what I've learned and give others a chance to do the same.

After my first transplant, I was thankful for the opportunities to help others, but mostly for the extra time I was told I would not get. I was grateful for days, but more so for even small moments.

Sunsets, full moons, shooting stars, trees and growth. Grateful for health and recovery. It made me reach out to others and support whomever, and however, and whenever I could and even gain the courage to become a mentor to others who were at the place where I was so lost and confused. I had a chance to give others what I did not have on my journey.

I did not interact with any other transplant recipients until after mine. My road pre-transplant was a lonely one to put it mildly, not to mention scary. I showed my gratitude by giving others what I did not have so they would not feel what I did.

By choosing this, I have been able to reach many and give those help and support when they needed it the most. Being grateful for struggle and pain, that has taken me to another level. Being grateful for the good things comes easy, but being grateful for the bad times or the hard days takes you to another level and opens up doors where you didn't even realize there was one.

In addition, being able to do this makes us more appreciative of the good things. Had I not attained silicosis fibrosis, my life would be way different, but if I could go back, I wouldn't change a thing because the way I live and see things and I thank God that it has all been worth it to make these realizations and implement them in my life. I can't be grateful enough that I'm still here to grow, evolve, and share with everyone in a helpful way.

Sometimes my helpful is kind of rough and real, and it's in those moments that I've learned to dial it back a bit because everyone is not like me, and everyone feels differently and is experiencing differently. I always say tough times do not last, but tough and faithful people do.

I know that is not the only way and I am grateful for the opportunity to learn from others, and I try to help. I am grateful for my Donors. For without them, I would be gone. A mere statistic to work related deaths, grateful that a complete stranger would be so grateful for their own life, that they'd be willing to give life as their last act on earth and for their families, for honoring their wishes, and for doctors and all medical staff.

For without them, these miracles would be difficult to pull off. I am grateful to God for his miracle and blessings bestowed on us. I am grateful for coming into my own as a Warrior and not being afraid to make my unheard-of ring loud and clear so others can do the same with theirs.

I am grateful for all those that had the courage to stay present in my difficult life, but also for those that showed their true colors and left. It is important to learn from everyone who crosses our paths, good or bad, to truly evolve, grateful to be able to throw negative in my fire and turn it into positive.

Mostly I am grateful for God's belief in me and for his love. When I was not able to love or have faith in myself, he did in me and for not leaving me when I forgot about him. As I traversed the dark side and not forgetting me through all those super scary moments when I was so close to death by strengthening me and protecting me. I have lived. I have died. I have failed when I tried and succeeded when I was dying and living the right way, so my gratitude for it all will only ever grow, not fade.

Chapter 16

My Donor and Donor Family

My first donor was 42 when she passed. I was also 42 at the time. She was a victim of domestic violence, a horrific, senseless act. She took a beating from a coward who left her and her son on a two-lane highway in the early morning of September 18th, 2011, in Nebraska.

Left on a dark road for dead another hero appeared. A nine-year-old son. He was in the back seat laying down asleep. As they were driving, she and the coward were in the middle of a conversation about her not wanting to be with him anymore. He then pulled over and pulled her out of the vehicle and she yelled to her son to run and hide.

He did just that and hid in a drainage culvert. The coward proceeded to beat her all in the head and face.

She was a beautiful woman, and he figured that if he couldn't have her, no one else would either.

After the beating, the coward took off down the road leaving a Mother for dead and a Son fearing his own death. As the Young Boy saw lights coming, he jumped out of the culvert and stopped the approaching car.

It turned out the lights belonged to a policeman's car. Shocked and surprised to see a young boy come out of nowhere from the darkness, the officer slammed on his brakes. The boy then told the police officer what had happened.

After the policeman helped him in the car, he began driving down the road. He saw a figure on the road and a closer look showed him a woman bleeding badly and left for dead by the afore mentioned coward.

As soon the officer saw it was the woman, he told the boy to lay down and not to look up in case the coward was still around. Also, I am sure he did not want the young boy to see his Mom like that.

He told him, "Don't look up, no matter what you do, stay lying face down."

Approaching her body, he drove past and began calling for help. Soon the area that was completely dark would be filled with lights and emergency vehicles.

The coward had taken off down the road. And of course he took the coward's way out. He ended up going into an open garage and hung himself. As cowardly an act as his previous one.

My Donor was taken to the hospital to save her life. With major head trauma, she needed immediate help. She was comatose and they were not sure that she would make it. Well as soon as her parents got the call, they booked a flight from New York to Nebraska. I am sure many of the emotions they experienced had a broad range and will always be unforgettable. Eventually she came out of the coma and began showing improvement. Everyone was much more optimistic now about her making it through this horrible and senseless tragedy.

About three weeks later she was told she could go home. Her parents drove her to Colorado. At home in Castle Rock, she kept improving so the optimism for her recovery was high. That sadly would not take place. She had an aneurism.

Because of the trauma she received to her head, she was now being rushed back to the hospital. This time nothing could be done. The trauma to her dead was too great and she was hooked up to life support machines. It was then that her family was informed that she was an organ donor, they never knew this. She registered her first license at the age of 16.

Her family, not wanting her to endure anything else contemplated not going through with it. After this family conversation, they decided that honoring her wishes was best and they proceeded.

Two things about this story. If her young son didn't have the courage to t jump out of the ditch and stop that car, she would have undoubtedly died. Then I would have died, most likely a few weeks later. As the surgeon explained to me after the surgery.

Second thing is, if my Donor Family would have stopped it, I would have more than likely died the next day or two. I was operating at 8% lung function for a year. There wasn't much left in the tank to continue on much longer. The whole family saved me, and I have nothing but eternal love for them all.

As the surgeon explained to me that I would not have lasted more than a couple more days, I realized God's perfect timing. There wasn't much left in the tank and God knew it. My donor saved 6 people from death that day.

Giving life was her last act upon earth, it doesn't get any bigger than that.

She was such a giving person her whole life and now she was doing it one more time in the most miraculous way. Like an ANGEL HERO. My ANGEL HERO.

This might sound strange to some, but others may understand. I used to see her when I was on the edge of sleep in the ICU. I could hear her name inside my head, then I would see this tall blonde woman in a long white dress. She would be walking away, then stop, turn around, look at me and smile a bit, then some tears would roll down her cheek and she continued her walk.

I couldn't figure it out until I spoke with her parents for the first time on the phone. They told me her name and I saw her picture on Social Media, but I already knew it, I had already seen her. It was about 7 months after the transplant that this phone call took place with my Donor Parents. When I saw her picture, I just blurted it out without realizing, "I've seen her before!"

Very surprised, her Donor Dad mentioned she had been to Santa Fe for a weekend and asked if I had seen her then. Once again, I blurted out, "I saw her in the ICU."

I described what I saw and couldn't hold back the tears as the raw power of the moment took me over. It took all of us over. Almost 9 months post-transplant, I was able to meet them face to face in Colorado. As they were needed there to handle their daughter's financial affairs regarding property and vehicles. Coming from New York was not easy for them, but many of their daughter's friends were looking forward to the time that they would have together and me coming to meet them was a bonus.

I can't tell you the nervousness, my heart was ready to jump out of my chest. As I drove up to my Donor's friend's house where they planned a dinner for her parents, myself, and many other close friends, I had no idea of the level of amazing I was about to experience.

As I walked up to the house, my Donor Parents came out to greet me at the front walkway. We hugged and immediately the tears began to fall.

They both put their hands on my chest and back from each side and asked me to just simply breathe deep.

Fully and strong I inhaled and exhaled several times. It was one of the most powerful and surreal moments in my entire life. After we gathered ourselves, we went inside to meet all the others that were there. Everyone there had one thing in common. We all deeply loved Michelle Stella.

Have you ever walked into a room of strangers and felt like you knew them for a lifetime?

Or walk into a house you've never been to, yet you felt so at home?

Well, that was my experience. The questions were plenty, Some funny, some curious and some really hard to answer.

I found out where my sudden interest in classical music and margaritas came from as well as the pig like snort I do when I start laughing too hard now. Trust me. They were as freaked out as I was.

These connections between donors and recipients are real. Yes, they may vary in degree but they do occur. These organs are all made up of cells and these cells hold memory. So, yes, it does occur.

Once I was in a support group meeting and a doctor said we wouldn't start doing things we had never done before out of the blue. I then raised my hand to ask a question.

"What kind of transplant did you have?"

Seemingly taken aback by my question, he replied that he had not been a recipient of any transplant.

I replied, "How would you know, then? I have connections like that, and when you say things like this, we question whether or not something might be mentally wrong with us. There is nothing wrong with us. We have someone else's cells that hold their memories in our body. Theirs."

Visually thrown off by all of this, he continued and eventually approached me at the conclusion of the meeting. He told me he would no longer include any of that in any presentation ever again and wanted to apologize. So many connections that I could go on about. They all made me realize that God was waiting for the right match, and he took her by the hand and led her to me and five others and the miracles of organ donation were on full display.

ANGEL HERO is what I call her, she is my first donor. Sadly, I do not know who my second donor is and every time something happens that never has before, I just look up in the sky at the heavens and say, "I see you my ANGEL HERO, I see you BRO.

I truly feel in my heart and know in my mind that he also had a rough life. But because he gave life as his last act on earth, he is now resting eternally in the kingdom of heaven.

Hopefully whenever my donor family is ready, they will reach out and when they do, it will be on God's time, like everything else in this story, sometimes even down to the last hour.

One day I believe I will meet my Donor Family, and they can tell me about him. While I don't know for 100% certainty that my donor was a man, I feel very strongly that was the case.

Mostly because I don't like doing dishes again, I no longer browse, and I can always find something to wear now when I am going out. If you can recall, after my first transplant, I really enjoyed doing dishes, I cried a lot more, I enjoyed browsing, and I could never find a thing to wear. These are not jokes people, this was real.

I really did those things and had hot flashes too. Yeah. I know it was real.

Now as I cry, I remember my Dad's words, "Crying is a human emotion and do not to be ashamed of it. It is not female or male, it is a human emotion. It takes a strong man to cry."

This was a man who could split logs of oak wood in half with one strike. He was very much a manly man.

I've done some out of the blue things with this transplant as well. One Saturday morning while at home, me and my wife had on some music. A song came on and I sang it word for word. Then my wife said, "That's a cool song, who sings it?"

I responded with a straight face as I was sweeping the floor. "I don't know, I never heard it before."

She looked at me oddly to say the least. She watched me as I sang it word for word and again, I told her that I had not heard it before. Then realizing how insane it sounded coming out of my mouth I stopped sweeping and walked over to my phone. It said, 'Leonard Skynyrd, The ballad of Curtis Lowe'

While I knew Leonard Skynyrd was a band, I had no idea who Curtis Lowe was. Or that he even had a ballad. I then looked back at her and said it again.

"I've never heard that before."

I got chills throughout my entire body, realizing what just had happened. The same thing happened when I heard a song by Chris Stapleton, called, "Death row."

I sang it word for word. There is no way I should know what the 'no good life way down here,' looks like. I've never heard that song before. And knowing I've never seen anything close to that with my eyes.

I felt deeply this song and every word of it. You don't know why and I don't know how these things happen. Like the time I put a rear naked choke hold on a guy in a bar when I was never trained to do so.

Also, many of the things that I was so good at when I was running the dark side, gave me so many questions. The time I felt most connected though, was on my road to redemption. And that was my relationship with Jesus. And giving everything to God in all I was doing. I am in no way saying that what I did was because of someone else. I take full responsibility, always have, always will. What I am saying is that some of those occurrences felt like connections like I had the first time around.

I pray for my donors and donor families every day because if it's this hard for me I can't imagine what the pain was like for my donors to fight long enough to save someone or for their families to lose these precious loved ones.

About four months after my second transplant, I started listening to old country music from the legends and I absolutely loved it because I felt it. It's hard to explain it sometimes. Singing was a lot of fun, almost like remembering old times, even laughing when the song was done. Again, kind of coming out of nowhere, I fully embraced it and enjoyed it to the fullest. I still do, just not as much now.

I can't stand ice in my drinks now, even when it's hot outside. I just say I'm allergic to it because somebody always has something wise to say. I order water without ice because I am allergic to it, or at least this is what I say. Something about it just hits me different now. I also developed a taste for sardines and artichokes. Never had them so I can't say I didn't like them, but I sure will eat some now. With the little hot sauce and crackers that works for me. The only person who made any sense of it to me was my Donor Dad John. He told me about the organs being made-up of cells and how they hold memory. Prior to that I thought I was losing my mind because of lack of understanding about it all. There was another thing he mentioned to \me about when I had talked to him about survivor's guilt and still calling them

Michelle's Lungs. For a long time, I was still calling them Michelle's lungs.

Well, for her one-year anniversary mass I flew to New York from New Mexico and spent a week with my Donor Family. I also went to a mass, one in New York, and one in Connecticut where my Donor Sister lives. I stayed in the house that she grew up in and to this day it's still some of the best sleep I've ever had. I slept in her room. It was like I was home but actually she was at home, at least part of her.

I dreamt of her and an elderly woman with her so happy hanging on to each other as they laughed so hard. I learned so much about this amazing woman and it made my journey take a whole new route as now I had a name and face to put to the story.

John heard me call them Michelle's lungs and he stopped me and said, "What did you say?"

I repeated myself and then he corrected me in a way that opened my eyes up to what I'd really been chosen to receive.

He said to me that if he gave me leather jacket for Christmas every time, he saw me after that he wouldn't ask 'hey Mark how is my leather jacket?'

"Of course not, it's a gift, that's why it's now yours. My Daughter gave you a gift and they are now yours."

I told him I was having a hard time because I felt like I didn't deserve them so why did I get them?

He told me people don't get blessed based on their judgments of themselves and of course she couldn't have known, but God did, and obviously God thought you did. I'm forever grateful for that man that day, and for him and my donor family every day.

I keep praying to have that again with my second but like everything else, it's on God's time.

She gave me her lungs, her family, friends, and her giving spirit, and a chance to continue being a helper like she was. My Donor Family has really made my journey so much better. I've gone a couple of times to stay with them and it's always amazing. My donor's sister, God bless her. she has lost her Sissy, but she definitely gained a Brother. I love you, Cindy. I love you, John and Peggy.

Through tragedy and broken heartedness, only organ donation can produce miracles and connections that last amongst those who were once strangers.

Many years removed from the very tragedy that brought us together we are still part of each other's lives forever.

For anyone who doesn't know your donor keep writing those letters and the chances of getting a response only increase and whatever it is you're asking for in prayer believe that it's already come to you and then it will.

It's hard now because for the last 8 years I have wondered about them so much that it is exhausting at times.

I know it's in God's time. I just have to leave all that for God to figure out and keep living my life because 8 plus years on a second double lung transplant is a great run, so I have much to be grateful for.

I can't thank my first donor family enough for accepting me and loving me the way they have, treating me like family always. These connections are special and I'm fortunate to be able to still call them up and tell them I love them.

I heard my Donors voice on a voicemail recording and it was like hearing an Angel speak, it was beautiful. I say prayers for both my donors and donor families daily of gratitude and for their souls because without them my unfulfilled life would have ended long ago with me leaving a huge tab to pay to the universe.

Now each day I have a chance to live a life of service to continue paying down that bill and continue to pay my rent here on earth with my good deeds to anybody I can.

I pray for my donor families and for their loss. Without Donors there are no recipients, there are no stories, there are definitely no miracles.

It all started when she was 16 and who knew 26 years later, she would be chosen to save many with the ultimate gift, The Gift of Life. She made a commitment to her lifestyle keeping her strong and healthy so that her donation would always be usable and viable. Able to save life by giving life.

My second transplant, I have made it 8 plus years now which is incredible considering the average for second double lungs transplant is less than two years.

I have now been in the transplant life for 13 years and as each day comes that I wake, I only become more and more grateful as I realize every single day is a miracle.

My gratitude for my worst days has really served as the fuel for my fire and a great measuring stick about how God's love and power has got me through 100% of my worst days.

Organ donors are Angels and Heroes all rolled into one. That's why I call them ANGEL HEROES.

Like I stated earlier, giving life as your last act on earth well it doesn't get any bigger than that. I always imagine donors going straight to heaven on a super-fast escalator. Straight to the top, no stops. Zooming to the pearly gates with everyone clapping and showing the most love possible for their great last act.

I see God leading them by the hand to claim their seat that's been prepared for them once they've earned it. I know God's timing has always revealed itself to me. The first time it was down to my last days, the second it was down to my last hour. The third one, my time ran out. And for reasons only He knows, he gave me that time back and brought me back from death on that cold steel operating table.

When you are that close to crossing over it's hard to keep that belief that an ANGEL HERO is coming.

It takes great faith and even greater discipline to keep fighting, to just breathe, to just make it to the next day. Sometimes all you can do is make it to the next hour but making it to the next hour is a must in order to continue the fight as a Warrior.

I mentioned survivors guilt earlier and I had a big case of it after my transplant. I'm talking about this with my Donor Dad, and he stated very clearly that I wasn't alive because she died at the hands of a coward. I was alive because of the life commitment she made to save others' lives. However, any of that came to be had nothing to do with me receiving the gift of life, only that God took my ANGEL HERO by the hand and led her to me and five others.

We were chosen to receive her gift, and we should feel good about it and not ask God why? I'm so grateful for this man, his knowledge, and great faith.

My Donor Family is a huge blessing in my life as is the Donor Family I don't know yet.

He told me it was two different things that were joined together, not one thing depended on the other, or that being the reason.

It's kind of hard not to say, why did this person die, and I lived? One thing happened and because of the circumstance's others were gifted life. Miracles at the feet of tragedy.

My Donor Parents have enlightened me so much, it truly is equal parts touching and incredible. I just keep believing that God is preparing all involved for when I meet my second donor family. Let His will be done. The meetings are difficult but the relationships that are possible can be amazing and enlightening.

You know the saying, "Don't forget where you come from?" Well in my case it's been a constant struggle to understand parts of this for the past 8 plus years.

I have a lot of really strong thoughts on it, but nothing has been confirmed. Whoever my second donor was, he was one tough person, and I can feel that because he picked up right where my first donor finished her fight. Showing gratitude and love has been healing for me and provides me with inspiration to produce good in their names even if God's the only one with that name.

DONORS

Without Donors, there is no story. There is no miracle. There are only so many more endings. To give life as your last act on earth just doesn't get any bigger than that in my opinion. They have said those exact words in a commercial about mine and all the other ANGELHEROES. Living Donors are so amazing as well and it's beautiful to see the connections that take place and grow.

When God finds a match, it will only be on God's time. My first Donor saved six people from death and 15 others who weren't facing death.

Michelle Stella gave me her lungs but with that she gave me so much more. She also gave a young man a heart who had been sick with his since birth. All he knew was hospitals and not feeling good doctors and meds and all that goes with it.

Like everything else in life, a decision like that comes at different times for everybody. We never know where that inspiration to do such a great thing can come from. Every Donor is an Angel hero in the on-deck circle waiting for their chance to hit the grandest home run of their life.

When that match is made somebody gets time, more life, more opportunities.

Don't get confused, though, we as recipients never really get our life back. We get life and a chance to live but everything we do has to be done in a new way even if we are grateful and fortunate enough to do some other things we did before transplant. It's a new life, a new normal, that the recipient lives. There are too many new things to add to for it ever to be the same again. The biggest that any giver can ever accomplish is giving life and time to another.

I've come to know quite a few Donor Families and living Donors, and I'm blessed to be able to see it from other eyes. As a matter of fact, the wonderful woman Renee who officiated our wedding is a Donor Mom. Her daughter was an Angel Hero. My friend Courtney who is a speaker as well is a Donor Mom because her teenage Son was an ANGELHERO to many.

Something tells me all these amazing people were givers and helpers their whole lives. I know some living Donors who gave anonymously and how amazing are they?

I know others who were matched after being checked and chose to save a life. I remember the doctor telling me before my second transplant what my chances of survival were. I told him if someone else had a better chance with the lungs give them to that person. I then said, take my good organs and give others extra time like I had. All my other organs were still good, but they wouldn't stay that way if I kept going like this. I didn't want to be kept alive just to suffer, deteriorate, and break everyone's heart along the way. I wanted my life to mean something and living on through them was more than what I was doing in that bed.

I wanted to be a helper and a giver, and I told him that if something happened inside our surgery, my wishes were the same. Save lives with my organs. I know they were good, and I'd be checking to make sure I was preparing in many ways.

I said this because about 45 minutes to an hour earlier I felt my soul trying to leave my body. I was as close as I'd ever been, but I wasn't scared because I hadn't seen death like I had the first transplant. That's what I'm talking about when I say everything happens on God's time. He took that Angel Hero by the hand and led him to me while me and my first Angel Hero fought to stay alive long enough to make it to that meeting.

I don't know who my second was, but I do know he was tough and ready for battle right from the start just like Michelle Stella, and just like me. Sometimes things come out of nowhere and make me wonder who my second donor was when I do things I've never done.

I've come just to accept them as gifts, these connections, instead of trying to understand it. After a while I just had to tell myself to stop trying to figure it all out and just go with it.

So many great stories that never would have taken place without the great and heroic Donors. Miracles not witnessed, more families hurting to no end, more sadness and grief. Which leads me to how special Donor Families are as well.

Allowing the possibility for miracles both from their tragedies and unthinkable pain is truly a beautiful act as well. Their grief and loss are heavy so hopefully their load is lightened knowing their loved ones lived on through others. Many bittersweet moments along the way and our journeys together.

Many of these moments happened at the transplant games of America. Watching me perform and complete because of their loved one's gift I hope was a gift to them. I didn't become a Donor until I was a recipient, and I really don't know why. I never really was aware of it with no education or awareness about it growing up. I was a clueless, I knew one man who had a liver transplant when I was sick but that was it. I had nobody really to reach out to that could relate to what I was going through.

Since the year of 2021, there was over 40,000 lifesaving transplants in the US and the list has grown from there to 106,000. So, differences are being made by people like Roxanne Watson in New York who just registered her 13000[th.]

So many lives being saved with more than a decade of yearly increases it only gives the possibilities of science bettering the whole process and increase as well. Their commitments are more lives being saved. Truth is, we need more Donors so the numbers of Donors and people on the list isn't so just proportionate.

Sign up events happen all over the country but the more awareness out there the more Donors we have to be ready to become somebody's ANGELHERO. I've donated but admittedly I need to do more. Sometimes I'm reminded of what it would be like without their gifts when I see a fellow Warrior has passed waiting on the list.

Around 20 plus people die a day waiting for their gift but I will never say they lost because they fought till the end as Warriors do. I would have died too and no doubt I had already cheated death a few times but the last time

I was down to my last hour. The miracle was bestowed on me with a full display of God's perfect timing. Donors are the gift that keeps on giving you gifts over and over until we finally realize that all that happens are just more gifts wrapped in that initial Gift of Life.

Having time with my grandson has been a gift I never saw coming because he wasn't even a thought when I got my transplant, but he is an extension of my daughter so I believed that I was fighting for him, too, back in 2015 and early 2016, way before he was even born. That little man is amazing he is like my shot of B12 whenever I see him. He fills me with energy and life I thank God for my family every single day. I thank God for Donors and Donor Families everyday and for the miracles that are organ donation.

Donor Parents John and Pegy

Chapter 17

Enjoying the Rewards

After all the struggles, pain, uncertainty, and recovery, it is important to remember not to overdo it and do it with all the recommended precautions. Staying safe and healthy is super necessary. If you want to continue making memories and enjoying the rewards.

It is hard, but it is not always sickness and doctors and clinics and as always, hopefully not hospitals. I am sure those hospital stays have happened to everyone. I am also sure they have all had extra time to enjoy these rewards.

I say rewards because of all the times we fight through to the next day, we have to make sure that we make time for these moments because it is a healthy reminder to do it in a safe manner. Sick kids and babies were the ones that really hurt my heart when I could not help them or hold them, but it is a super easy way to catch something.

I hear coughing anytime I was in a store or a crowd, I was masked up and headed the other way.

I have been doing that whole mask and hand sanitizer thing for a while now, but sometimes I have been in restaurants and bars where I did not have it on. Those were the dumb days, the lost days, my bar days are way over with. I use it more now because I want more memories and rewards for the days, months, and years to come.

Battling for another 24 while wondering if you can even survive the day you are in is taxing on every part of you but we battle on. These battles are extreme and will leave even the strongest with some PTSD post-transplant.

I have been fortunate enough to be able to make some funny and awesome memories in the midst of those battles and that is a bonus. As I have said, it is great to laugh. Great memories can even be better if you can laugh at your own stuff. These are also rewards and they are big ones that keep you going in your most unsure times.

Unsure about the meds, infections, rejections. When you are going, where you are going, how did you get through where you were? Uncertainty. Uncertainty in the beginning is in abundance and its key to not become the "if" person and get swallowed up by it.

After so much time in the smack dab middle of a fight of the fiercest ever, it is necessary to have these moments. The rewards. One of the biggest rewards was when I entered and competed at the Transplant Games of America.

This experience was eye opening and life changing on a whole other level. I had no idea what to expect. All I knew was I was on a mission to get there and compete. Competing in sports has been part of my life since second grade. Competing, well, let us just say longer than that.

Sports taught me so much about life that is relevant and relatable. Working with different people all attempting to complete a common goal can be amazing and if you can transfer that to work, it is even better. It is not focusing on oneself or on the possible future competitors. The best teams, are the ones that have the people filling roles according to their strengths while developing their weaknesses. The successfully consistent have mastered this. Putting personal accolades and egos aside, it always makes for unique and enlightening feats, some that will be remembered many times over with laughter and gratitude.

At times, sports and my coaches taught me many things I still utilize in my daily life and when I am dead center in a battle of the transplant variety. Many times, in rehab, I would envision myself deep in my mind doing those sports workouts that you were glad about when they were over and where you looked at each other and you wonder how you had not fainted.

These visualizations would power me through many workouts as I tried to harness it more each time and I would go back to these workouts in my mind from when I was a young student athlete. As I sat there in a hospital gymnasium, in a pulmonary rehab program fighting for my life, I would channel that energy I received from this visualization of returning back to a workout and my high school and collegiate days and use that to its fullest.

In my current situation where I was suffering from silicosis fibrosis, the running of football stadium steps for two hours, the four-hour practices, the two a day and even three a day at times in upper levels of sports practices. The 12 miles I ran because I was thrown out of practice, the hundreds of laps and sprints I was channeling is what it took to get those workouts done, in order to get value from the workouts that I was doing as I was preparing for the fight of my life.

You are constantly working to get somewhere. Well, on another level it kind of sounds like preparing ourselves for competition through training. The opponent is death of course, so we fight even harder when the fight gets harder. I know respect and draw great amounts of inspiration and motivation from some upper tier warriors. Even when the odds are down or against you, true warriors will never quit. That is why it is important to enjoy the rewards.

Every Warrior should. It is our fuel for the next fight. The Transplant Games of America was one of the most incredible experiences of my life. From the opening ceremonies, it takes you on an emotional and competitive emotional journey of a competitive nature. I saw things that moved me, changed me and inspired me to do more with this transplant than just receive it.

I knew even before the transplant that it was not just about me getting better; it was also about me helping others with their journey. The transplant games were a beautiful example of that. I saw 80-year-olds running. I saw men and women giving it their all in basketball and volleyball. I saw children running and smiling, which brought me to my little buddy from Virginia, Mr. John Eitzel.

This young man did one of the most incredible things I have ever witnessed in sports. It was the 50-yard dash, and the little guys and girls were excited to run. I stopped and watched from the side as I had just competed in the long jump. They lined up, the starter gun went off, and there they went as determined as they could possibly be. One kid though, he got a good start, and he was way off in front of everybody. It was as if he was shot out of a cannon or something.

As he was approaching the finish line though, he looked back. Then he just stopped, and he made a complete 180 and he started going the other way. Well, I did not see it at first because it was really far back, but another kid was doing the race in a walker. He was way behind, and all of the other kids had finished except for him and another kid. Yes, you got it. My buddy from Virginia, Mr. Eitzel, is about ready to win first place. He turned around and went back to support another.

Instead of crossing the finish line, he went back and helped the kid in the walker. He gave up the gold medal because he saw someone he wanted to help. He did not care about the medal. He just wanted to be a helper. Talk about inspiration.

I do not think there was a dry eye in the stadium. I knew mine weren't. This was amazing and certainly foreign to my eyes. I had never seen that before, especially from someone so young. To have that capacity to care and love was one of the most special moments. Great job Mom and Dad! You raised a good one.

Very few things in sports have impressed me that much. He would have won, he gave up the gold, but that act won him the athlete of the games and in that act I realized what my life as a transplant recipient would be and the role I would be stepping into as a helper, a giver and a servant.

I participated in track and field, basketball and I bowled with my Donor Mom. That was so much fun. Bowling with her and having my Donor Dad coach me was another incredibly special moment. In addition, when I played basketball, they watched every second of those two games and it truly was an honor to compete again because of my Angel Hero, their daughter Michelle.

The first game we won, and I scored 30 points, and the second game, 36, but we lost. One win and one loss and just like that, we were out of the competition. I was not mad though and I will tell you why.

I wanted to win a medal badly so I could give it to my Donor Parents. Well, I gave them something, not a medal though, but they were able to watch me do what I used to do in college with their daughter's lungs in my body. I was only nine and a half months post-transplant. The men that I had on my team were men that I will hold the greatest respect for, always . A teenage boy, two older men and a swimmer. They did not know basketball, but they played so I could play. They were way out of their element, but they did not even blink when it came to competing.

They were all guarding players bigger than them, stronger than they were, faster than they were. One of the reasons I scored 66 points in two half court three on three games with 15-minute running halves was partly I had college experience, and I could score, but also it wasn't that I was ball hogging, it's just that they told me to shoot the ball every single time because that was the only chance we had. It was an incredible experience, so shoot the ball, I did. I felt like a kid out there. It was awesome.

I quickly found out it was not one of those feel good competitions though, where everyone is friends and plays nicely together. These people wanted that hardware around their neck very badly, so they were playing very hard. I found out when my friend from Indiana who's built like a refrigerator with a hairy back gave me a shot in my back with what felt like a piece of wood.

I turned around and I saw the huge shoulder that looked like a bowling ball covered in hair and I said, okay, this is a real game.

Then I gave him one of those joker smiles and went to work and we ended up with a victory and another chance to play. Little did I know we were facing the defending champions with four NCAA Division One Athletes. They were not small guys either. These guys could move and play the game on a high level. I never met a tall guy I did not want to play against though, and at only 5'10" I walked around and played as if I saw a seven-footer in the mirror in the morning. I believe they were at a disadvantage, and I played hard every game. We were obviously outmatched and lost 38 to 54.

My guys had not even played high school and one of them was still in high school, but they were never afraid. It was amazing because I know I could not go to their events and do the same thing they did. That is why I have the utmost respect for these men and the rest of Team Rocky Mountain.

I was kind of down after because we were out of the tournament and my Donor Mom and Dad walked up behind me and placed their hands on my chest and back and as they did the first time I met them.

I started breathing in and out and as we all cried, I said, "I wanted to win it for you guys and give you the medal." My Donor Dad then said, "You've given us so much already, Mark."

I was able to win a bronze medal in the long jump, but they insisted I keep it, and I jokingly asked them if it was because it was a bronze? Then we all burst out laughing. Bittersweet moments. I even ran in the 5K that opened the games. It was a rough five days, but it was five of the most awesome days of my life and I am so grateful to experience it.

I left Grand Rapids, Michigan wanting to start training for Houston. The things I saw, the people I talked to and became friends with, well, they will always have a special place in my heart.

In Houston, I received two awards, a bronze and one silver for long jump and basketball. I put that silver medal around my lung Brother Jaime's neck before they closed his coffin. We always talked about playing ball at the transplant games of America, but he was not able to get off the oxygen, but I did get to bowl with him. He bowled a great game with oxygen on and me, not so much. Those days with my Lung Brother I will cherish forever, and always be grateful for the time God gave me with this incredible man, Jaime Munoz, I love you Brother. The rewards we fight for that we do not even know are coming will always be a reminder how God is always working way ahead of us.

One of the biggest ones, if not of my transplant life, but my entire life was the blessing I have in my wife. She reminds me of two women, one young, one old they are the strongest I know. My Daughter and my Momma. Handling adversity and awful times with the most grace and dignity is what makes them so similar. Much like my Nana and Grandma.

She impresses me daily, quietly challenges me to be better than I used to be and works together with me for our future. Much of what it's taken me to write this has been inspired by my love for her and the courage it took to take a chance on a very broken man. She is the biggest reason this story is still going so good.

Over five years ago at this time, I went for a beer with a friend. What happened that night would forever change my life. I met the most beautiful woman and her lovely curly curls and instantly I knew because I could feel my energy pulling towards hers trying to join together. I calmly took a step back and then lightly excused myself to the restroom. My energy ball was all over the place, so I got in that small bathroom, locked the door and proceeded to calmly punch myself, Smack dab in the energy ball as hard as I possibly could.

Yes, people, I fully gut checked myself hard, like very hard and then proceeded to have a conversation with my energy ball. I explained that we'd be taking it nice and slow and then I washed my hands, and I began to return telling my energy ball, "You don't have a good track record and you've gotten me into the wrong places places with all the wrong women, so now we're going to take it nice and slow and do this my way."

So, I proceeded to return to the where this woman was, and I said goodnight to this beautiful vision. I knew if I did not say goodnight at that moment and immediately go home, that there was a high chance that I would ruin anything that I could ever have with her. She was glowing, brighter than she would ever know. I went home and I did not mess it up.

Sooner rather than later we got ahold of each other, and we went out and we have been together ever since. However, that was dangerous, me leaving that night because had she not agreed to give my friend her number, maybe I might have missed the blessing of a lifetime. Without her, I might be dead or in prison.

So, speaking of incarceration, when I got out, she was the only one waiting and she could have said, I am done, but she has never given up on me nor me her and she is of my greatest blessings. I was able to marry this blessing of a woman on October 10th, 2021, and one of the biggest reasons I'm a stonemason again and doing the work necessary to reach as many as I can. She did not give up on me, she did not judge me and when I fell, she did not tell me how to get back up. She just reached her hand out and helped me to stand again, allowing me to naturally see the capabilities we have to turn this into something to bring about a positive change.

I am not sure how one goes through life without seeking the rewards of their hard work or victory in their battles. When you fight as hard as we do, it is so necessary to enjoy the rewards and benefits we experience on the other side of the battle. It does not mean that the battle is over, it just means it is time to rest and recover and enjoy yourself for those brief moments before we encounter our next fight. My rewards have come a plenty with all the ones that have given me their all on this journey, recognizing I have given my all for them as well. Every day we awaken is a blessing, a reward, and an opportunity to make a difference in someone else's life besides our own. As I look around me, I only see the truest ones to still be here with me on my journey because of their love and support and action. These Trues have made it our journey.

It truly is our journey. If we look at things in a certain way or reach a higher level of understanding, we even evolve into the belief that our struggles and pain are rewards. For our many days in battle, some of us should not even be here to experience these struggles and pains and that is why we must look at them in this manner. Those, my friends, are the ones that build us up into the fiercest.

We are the most loving and understanding Warriors on the battlefield, God helped us turn our pain into power, our heartaches into helpfulness and hope for others and our traumas into triumphs and teachings for that are in need.

These are the words I developed to help me with moving past my pain and struggles and because I am grateful for these things that most cannot find gratitude towards. I have been able to move to a new place where these things serve as my positives and never my negatives. Again, the things that once hindered me now power me and fuel my fire. Turning negatives into positives, giving me back twice the power. This also has become a reward for me because at one time in my life these things set defeat in motion. Now they empower me tremendously and provide me with all the strengths I need to keep battling for more days.

When you push through with positive thinking and action in the midst of the dark times or struggles, what we get back in terms of getting what we need to continue and grow is immeasurable, but we can also go the other way quickly with the wrong ones.

Energy is everything and we will decide what type of energy we choose to put into our endeavors. You get what you give truly is the thing we focus on, and we draw what we exude and what we exude is taken in by all those around us or to all those with access to us. These battles are never just about us and never should be. There is always somebody watching who is part of the struggles, pains, and the rewards. Why on Earth would we fight so hard if there were no reward at the end?

It is ridiculous, right? What is the point of battling as warriors if we cannot enjoy our victories? Being in some of the fiercest battles, I have finally come to realize how important the rewards and celebrations truly are.

How do we refuel for the next one? When you make it out of the end of something difficult or it may seem impossible, the best thing to do is show gratitude and take a little time to enjoy all your hard work, dedication and perseverance has produced.

We can never get too comfortable because our battles are many and the next one awaits around the next corner. Always enjoy the rewards after the hard-fought battles. Always. This is a way of thinking. This way of thinking should be for everyone, not just transplant recipients or people experiencing pain or struggle.

Why would we work so hard just for the sake of working hard? Nobody should ever just work hard. You and nobody should ever just work your fingers to the bone because in the end all you end up with is bony fingers, unusable, bony fingers. Enjoying our victories, recharges us, revitalizes us for our future battles, and provides us more insight on how to take on our upcoming battles. While in the middle of these battles, we have the opportunity for major growth, and we have another chance to continue, or we have another chance to continue stunting that growth.

Depending on our choices, I can honestly say I would never be even close to that warrior I am now, If I was asking why me, I would not be enjoying the rewards of my commitment to my battles. When we push through fear, doubt, pain and negativity, the possibilities are endless. Once we have developed the ability, we accomplish things we were given next to nothing for a chance. It strengthens us in every way and makes the unheard of seem like something very attainable.

Belief in yourself after coming out of something nobody gave you a chance to is empowering beyond words. You literally go from what is happening here to I see what you're doing here, God, and thank you for showing me what lies within me when I have faith in you and belief in myself. Never risk dislocating your own shoulder, patting yourself on the back, but always remember to celebrate yourself and enjoy the rewards of being a true warrior, but do it in a humble manner so you can continue being a hardworking and helpful warrior. To hear voices or see the smiles of loved ones can be measured to waking up on a Christmas morning. Hearing my Grandson and Daughter talking and getting ready to open presents is one of the best rewards for all the hard work and pain I have been through.

I would go through it all again just to have those moments. These are the very moments that I visualized over and over getting myself to the point of being able to enjoy these moments and rewards for spending so much time in battle. Right now, as I am writing this, I can hear my grandson so excited about opening presents and hugging his Elf Mr. Figgy Smalls, the Elf on the shelf. Wow. Now that is a reward.

Chapter 18

The Who and the What

When you are fighting to continue your life, you must first decide why you are fighting. Fighting with no purpose or logical reason truly is a waste of time, not something you should do when you are running out of it.

My initial reason was my Daughter. She was just a teenager with her whole life ahead of her. When I got sick and for being so young, she sure carried herself beyond her years. She would ask questions, watch transplant videos on new procedures and surgeries with me. I know she must have been terrified, but she never let it show. She became my source of strength to not give up and she might not have even known it.

The thought of leaving her here on this earth without me was enough for me to put aside the pain and the heartache of the massive dose of life interrupted and fight like I never had before. I know this experience left her with some good memories but also with some that were awful and devastating. In times like these, it is important to remember to take it one moment at a time because things can change so quickly, and they do.

When I was a teenager, I was faced with something similar. My junior year, my Dad got sick and had to be hospitalized. It was the middle of the basketball season, and he was my Coach. A man so strong in every way. It was so hard seeing him like that. How could Superman be lying in a hospital bed? I felt so alone in those days. He was and is still the strongest man I will ever know. It was the biggest test of my young life and the fear I had going through the rest of my life without my hero was unbearable to even fathom when I found my daughter in that same situation, I knew I had to show her how much she meant to me as well as teach her how to never quit.

Regardless of the severity of the situation, I really believed that I was teaching her the last lesson in my life and the most important one when faced with insurmountable odds. It can be easy to give up, but I would not, and was not about to do that with the eyes of the most important person in my life on me. My Dad showed me how to do it and I was blessed to be able to do the same for her.

When you love someone that much, it is not hard to decide how far you will go for them. The best creation I'll ever be a part of was watching my every move and if I was going to be successful at this, I'd have to put aside all of my pain and hurt and show her that I'd fight with every last bit of me to stay here with her. I know she was scared. Heck, I was scared. How could I not be? How could she not be?

At 14 years old, you are told your dad is dying. Anyone would be devastated. I thank God every day for my daughter and that she is way beyond her years. She handles things better than people do twice her age and I am blessed She calls me Dad. When you see that kind of sadness in your child's eyes, it rocks you to your core because all you want to do is fix it and be there for them.

Well, all I could do was fight to stay alive and indeed, I did, like the Warrior I was born to be. I gained so much mental toughness throughout this ordeal, and I am so grateful for that. When the body is not good, the mind and spirit have to be at their all-time strongest.

How do you fight knowing you are losing? You keep fighting because it is not over. That is how you find your reason and purpose and never let anything change that. When your reason is your only child, it is easy to wake up again and battle even if you do not survive; you have shown those that you love the most that they were worth all the pains and the battles hard fought.

I do not know how others come to the decision of quitting. It must be a horrible pill to swallow, but I know everyone has his or her reasons for fighting or choosing not to. I could not bear the thought of my Mari living her young life without me, so I fought, and I fought until I did it. It is hard to do it once, much more the second time.

That second time she was older, but it was much harder because the first time I was not on my deathbed, the second was so different and considerably more difficult.

I was living in Phoenix waiting for the call that might not come and she was in Santa Fe at our house, and it came. I cannot imagine the loneliness and uncertainty she felt, but she never showed it. I know it was an extremely difficult time of her young life, but she remained solid and strong in every way.

She never broke down in front of me or let me get down. Throughout the entire ordeal, she was with me. When I got the call and I knew God was working, my baby girl had become a force of nature when many would have crumbled, she became stronger.

Having that talk with her before surgery and the possibility of me not making it were the most difficult moments of the journey and my life. Telling her I loved her maybe for the last time, communicating my expectations of her and how she would make sure her future kids would know all about Grandpa Mark and what I expected of her for the rest of her life.

The things we both learned about life were incredible. I was fighting for my Mom and Dad too, but it was different, and it was with my Daughter. I felt like my job was not completed and I could not just let that be. Every time I wondered if I had anything left for this fight, I thought of her and I would instantly have my answer.

There is no emotion bigger than my love for my Daughter. She changed my life and gave me the opportunity to become a real man and Dad. She saved me a long time ago. How could I say that this is too hard, or I cannot handle it? I could not and I would not, but she will always be my reason and my purpose because she did not abandon me ever as the others had before. I will never give up on her ever.

I know many days my body would tell me it couldn't or wouldn't or didn't want to anymore, but my mind and my spirit were strong, and I wouldn't be chased from this fight. I remember her face as the medical jet started to taxi down the runway, an image I will never forget and used as a constant reminder about why I am doing this. Her beautiful face with tears running down her cheeks and the look of uncertainty gave me the fuel I needed for a long, tough battle. She is my everything and you just do not give up on that. You just do not.

When your reason and purpose are that special, the fight takes on a different look because you will literally do what you have to in order to have these moments and memories no matter what it is.

The second time after surgery, she stayed in my room with me for three weeks straight, sneaking showers in the bathroom and eating from the cafeteria and vending machines while sleeping on a tiny little couch. She never wavered and helped as much if not more than the aides. I will never forget those days for they were the ones I watched my little girl transform into an adult woman. She was my solid rock. During that time, her and my Momma kept me going with their care, love and strength.

The first one, my Dad was with me, so he and my mom did everything to get me back to healthy again. Those were the hardest times I have ever experienced with my Parents and my Daughter, but they were definitely some of the best growing and evolving in the midst of loss and tragedy. It is empowering beyond measure and belief.

Although I did not have my Dad the second time to help me get to that point, one of the things that kept me going was thinking about the next time I would see my Dad. I never wanted that first question to be "Why did you quit? Son, I never taught you that."

He always told me he never raised a quitter, and I am fortunate he did not. After my Dad passed about two and a half years into my first transplant, my reason and purpose became crystal clear, and I've not looked back and I'm so thankful that my Dad never let me learn to quit. Truly an amazing man. I made it by still using the things he taught me and that is how I honor him. During the second transplant, I could feel his presence in many moments.

My 77-year-old mama at the time was a super rock star Hero. She did everything for me for many months.

She truly is the strongest woman I will ever know. Her faith unshakeable and her love immeasurable, she always says, "I love you more," and she will always be right. I wish everyone in the world could have a Mom like her. My Parents are heroes in my eyes, and I thank God for choosing me to be their Son.

When a person tries to fight without reason or purpose, usually they will not be successful and without God, the fight is impossible to win. My Parents and my Daughter were my reason, and because of that, I have experienced more victories than defeats in this ongoing battle for my life.

"In my life's book nowhere will it ever read, He gave up and quit, not even one time, because quitters always lose and never win."

I wholeheartedly know that when I see my Dad again, he will not ask me why I quit for that will never be an option because Warriors never quit.

My Daughter is kind of like another Parent now, making sure I am doing what I have to and letting me know when I do not. She has had the single most effect on me, becoming the Warrior I have become.

Fighting is never easy, but when you know your reason and purpose for it, things become clearer and it's easier to set your game plan up to fight for your life. Truth is we all have to fight for something. Find that reason and purpose to be successful. If one does not know whom, what, or why they are fighting, how can they figure out how? These days I have been able to experience this, and it has been truly life changing.

Graduations, birthdays, Grandchildren being born, and watching your own baby blossom into a great and awesome adult is a reward like no other. Getting married and making comebacks are also some of the greatest rewards for this Warrior.

My Wife, my Momma, my Daughter. They have given me so many moments because of their love and strength. I cannot ever thank them enough.

Same goes for my Dad. This has all made me realize that being tougher than anyone gave me credit for and not giving up because of the odds has allowed me to be present in the greatest moments in my life when living on extra time. There is no room for waste of time, energy or emotion, but only time for battling like the fiercest of Warriors and loving with the biggest of hearts so you are not on your deathbed feeling that you left so much undone.

When your reason and your purpose are true and genuine, then your fight will be of the highest caliber. Nobody will ever be able to convince you otherwise. I am thankful for all of this because without it, we would most definitely be different people with different mindsets.

Thinking about every little thing that happens is the worst thing ever. Our struggles reveal our strengths, and I will say it as long as I am here. I am so grateful. My struggles, battles and pain have empowered me and strengthened me beyond my own belief and measure. I am grateful I did not let them crush me. Define me and defeat me.

Silicosis fibrosis has taken a lot from me, but it will never take my soul, my belief in God, myself, and God's love. It will never take my Warrior spirit and will never define me as sick and unable to be present in my life and my loved one's lives. People used to ask me how long I had been sick, I would get mad, and I would say, "I'm not sick. I just need a double lung transplant, but I am not sick."

Many times, when we are in the midst of these types of battles, we forget who is watching, something we must never do. If we quit, then maybe unconsciously we are giving others permission to do the same. When we fight against insurmountable odds, we show others that it is very possible. Quitting is a horrible thing because when you start, it is a last resort, but the more you do it and the more you choose it, the easier it gets and the more quickly it becomes your first choice. Maybe it starts with a game or a team, then school or a job, then friends and family, maybe a relationship.

At that point, it becomes so easy to quit on yourself and progress in steps. Small ones at first, gradually turning to large ones and before you know it, everything has a built-in excuse and is on the table. We might not know how to win the battle or the race yet, but that does not mean that you give half effort or give up entirely. We keep pushing to excel with the belief that our own reason and purpose are out there. It is our responsibility to find them both and cultivate them into the strongest possible.

Quitting is so easy, and fighting is not. After all is said and done and the dust settles, whom of you will decide to be Warriors? Never be quitter. Warriors never quit because that is when you lose in life and then you realize you are not even worthy of being called a Warrior any longer.

Whom will you decide to be? I look back on those days as a reminder that I could easily be there again. That is just the nature of transplants because they do not last forever. Nothing does. Through these battles and challenges, we find a version of ourselves we never knew existed.

I used to think I was tough, and I could handle anything, but the difference now is that I know I can and that is a huge difference.

We are all Warriors innately. It just takes different things to bring it out of us and as I laid in the hospital bed, the words of my Dad have never rung truer.

"Either you get busy dying or get up and answer the bell and fight like you never have before to keep on living and even if you do not make it, wherever you show up next, you will show up as a warrior and not as a quitter."

When you are on the verge of quitting, it's important to know that your breakthrough is so close, it is closer than you think and can happen at any moment, so do not quit right before you're about to receive the reward.

Had I quit, I would have missed so much and many of the happiest days of my life. I prayed to make it to those special days and now I pray to make it to more because my reason and my purpose are the fuel that powers me is this fight. The power of love and prayer can make the impossible into the unheard of and I will never forget that because now it is all possible and that is why I am still here trying to make a difference.

Just like my Mom and Dad, Daughter, and my Wife made a difference in my life so that I would have a chance to do this for others. Show others that the impossible is not that far from becoming your truth. In reality, making the unheard of be heard loud and clear around the world, we can only make that happen with belief in ourselves in everything we do.

Sometimes life interrupted has some great-unexpected benefits, the ones that can drive you beyond any destination you ever imagined. For the majority of my life, I felt I was just an ordinary person living this life, but life interrupted showed me I could be one. I can be one in almost 8 billion with the right mindset, game plan, an unshakable faith, what has supposed what was supposed to be my last days have led to my very best days and giving me the opportunity to have many more impactful days. I can be one, the one showing everyone nothing is impossible with God.

Just B.R.E.A.T.H.E. & Believe

Daughter Mari and Me and my Grandson Jax

Chapter 19

Caregivers

A very important part of this equation is the caregiver's role. Without these awesome people, I believe many would pass quickly. These are Heroes as well. It is a selfless role and one that requires great strength, understanding and patience. Those who fill this role are, in my opinion, Angels of Mercy as well as nurses. Theirs is a difficult role to fill and not everybody can do it.

Watching a person slip closer to death each day is hard and challenging to say the least. Trying to keep someone going to get a transplant or helping them recover after transplant is a job that is not for everyone. There are many stories of people just giving up and leaving their sick spouses or partners, and they are all equally heartbreaking to those who have been left like this.

Trust me when I say they did you a huge favor for showing their true colors. That is why the ones that embrace this role are in my book. Angels of Mercy. It is difficult to see someone you love, decline, struggle, recover, or eventually pass. I have to say I was blessed to have the caregivers I did, and I believe it is directly related to how the journey goes.

My first transplant, my Parents came to Denver for three months to take care of me. They had already done plenty before we went to Colorado, but now they were taking it full time, 24 hours a day with all the responsibility and the tidal wave of emotions, and those are the only guarantees when stepping into this role after transplant.

It is a one day at a time kind of thing when anything can change in a heartbeat. The times I spent with my Parents going to clinic or pulmonary rehab gave us the opportunity to become closer, gain more understanding and compassion, and learn who we really were at our cores. I saw how hard it was for them to see me like this, but never once did they put their fears, anxieties, frustrations or doubts in front of their commitment, and this is just another reason why I call them my Heroes.

Before the transplant, I remember my Momma cleaning everything top to bottom so I wouldn't get an infection, cooking meals and doing the laundry and most importantly, praying. My Dad was there to take me to appointments with the doctors, to clinic visits, pulmonary rehab and in my appointments, asking all the right questions and making sure he and the doctors were doing what was needed to get me on the way to recovery to healing. My Momma and Dad were a team operating with precision like they had done before. Well, actually they had, both of them were caregivers for their Parents at the last stages of their lives.

I am sure they never imagined they would be my caregivers, but when it came up, they stepped in and stepped up like the great Parents they have always been. Without them, I had no idea what I would have done. They selflessly put their lives on hold to make sure mine had a chance to continue. So many moments every day where their acts of love are truly what kept me going. The only time I saw my Dad get mad or frustrated was when we got lost for a brief moment. I do not think I could have done it with anyone else.

I remember one time I was struggling to get in a good position while sitting in a recliner and my Dad wanted to help, but I told him I could do it. After a few minutes of struggle, I was able to get centered and comfortable and then I heard what I knew was my Dad crying behind me, so I asked, "What's going on over there?"

He told me that he was so sorry for being so hard on me, and being so tough on me when he was raising me and being so demanding of me when he was my basketball coach.

I then told him, "Don't ever say that again, Dad. It was as if you could see into the future and you knew I would have to be one of the toughest people to walk this earth to survive, and you raised me as such. Do not ever say that again because I would not be here with a chance had you done it differently."

I know it was hard for my Momma too and that is why she kept herself so busy all the time. I have to say, I have the greatest Parents and many of you out there know what I am talking about because you do too. The second time I got sick, I was in a relationship, and I knew it was shocking to see how fast things changed, but this person stepped up and she made sure that I had a chance to get another transplant. I will never forget that, and I will always be grateful even though we did not make it, her efforts kept me alive and still gave me a chance.

My Daughter also stepped-up big time becoming a great young woman in front of my eyes. As I've seen many other children do this great act of love, a role where it's absolutely necessary for the caregiver to make sure and care for their selves first because it's so demanding to have a ringside seat to a pretty crazy show and taking responsibility of aftercare is huge.

Undoubtedly words will never do justice to these selfless blessings we call our closest loved ones, the ones that stepped into that role, Heroes that facilitate success of the miracle.

We as recipients are eventually grateful for every single one because they have basically all been about your recovery and after being discharged from the hospital, we are weak and vulnerable. I have seen families pack up and go as a unit, relocate and even homeschool their kids because they are out of state long term.

Staying together from the beginning throughout transplant recovery and life after transplant, still one of the most amazing things I've witnessed on my journey to be blessed to be a witness and eventually part of spouses doing it all with little to no help. Through the worst of circumstances with little hope for success, only to eventually get to those great days. The best of days.

Parents that do it for their kids of all ages are brave and do anything to care for their own siblings, putting everything on hold to keep theirs alive and healthy, and sometimes it's those that are friends that feel more like family. They are all amazing. These facilitators of success in this miracle that transplantation provides, they are all amazing, these facilitators of success in this miracle of transplantation.

My first time I witnessed a family in the clinic visit, I was blown away. The Kids Club brought cookies for the staff before Christmas, and when I reflected on the overall experience, I prayed that I would know that beautiful family forever. I had the greatest in my Parents' post-transplant as well as my Daughter the second time. I had some great ones too that helped me stay alive to get to my second one. Those days before I left for Phoenix, I knew all that had been done to get me there.

Without these caregivers, I would never have made it so grateful for everything and everyone. I was blessed with that this time because it had to be unimaginably awful to watch it play out.

My deterioration was mind boggling because it was fast helping me get away from the quitters in Colorado to the very special place. I was at the St. Joe's in Phoenix, Arizona, and getting there was the biggest of blessings. I feel like I could do a whole book on the people of this institution. I know something brought me there, and I am sure my caregivers knew this too. Helping me make distance from quitters and join up with the ones who are willing to fight with me was God's work. God was guiding everybody, especially my caregivers.

I know it is the toughest of roles to step into and even tougher to stay in. I have heard where spouses or significant others leave when someone gets a diagnosis, it happens more than you think, as well as abuse. It is horrible, but it does happen.

At the Transplant Games of America, I met some of the greatest caregivers doing whatever it takes their loved one to be able to experience and enjoy the extra time. Caregivers sometimes forget to give some to themselves though. They were too caught up or consumed by being a caregiver.

It is very hard to help someone if you are not taking care of yourself too, you will be weakened and unable to do your best. You cannot do it for somebody and then not do it for yourself. Self-care is mandatory. It is not good to always have a front row seat on this journey, so we as recipients should remind them to take those moments as well. Step away, recharge and rest. Anyone involved will forever be changed. That is a given. Anyone taking on this role is a helper on a different level and can only be described as courageous and brave.

The ones that bring you what you need, not only in the form of food, water, and medicine, but they bring you all you need in all parts of your life, mentally, spiritually, emotionally as well. For those other parts is necessary to get the body back to where it needs to be in order to heal, progress and strengthen.

From my caregivers to the ones I have witnessed, do it. I know it takes a very special person to take on this role and all its responsibilities in a manner that promotes healing, recovery and a return to life's daily activities.

The caregivers that never get to see these are the ones that need prayer, support and love. They see the end and it undoubtedly changes them seeing the end of their loved one's life cycle.

These are angels as well, guided to do great things for others in the midst of their battle. As I speak of these great people, I willingly take this role and excel in it. There are those that do not and are reluctantly doing it. I pray for those doing it that can't or don't want to because they truly are missing out on the most special times that can be possible. When one's anxieties and frustrations carry over into the level of care they are providing. It is good for nobody involved, especially the patient. Resentment takes over and eventually when a person passes, the guilt sets in.

When a person passes, the guilt can be overwhelming. Being selfless and putting their lives on hold is surely a commitment that is like a gift because without these Earth Angels, we, the ones needing them, would have little chance of success, survival, and our gratitude is forever strong and I know from experience that being a caregiver for my Momma in the last phase of her life was one of the greatest blessings of my life. Being able to give her back what she had given me, being able to help her out in situations where she had helped me out when she was my caregiver, and I was on my deathbed. Truly a blessing and it was truly a gift.

Chapter 20

Warriors

This part is dedicated to the ones who helped me become who I am as a recipient and a Warrior.

When I first was diagnosed with silicosis fibrosis, I was told only a transplant would save me. I did not know anyone I could turn to that had one. I needed one and I did not know anyone at all. Where would I gain knowledge and understanding and whom would I go to for help or support before transplant?

All I learned about the process came out of books. It was not until after the transplant when I left the hospital that these awesome Warriors would present themselves to me as mentors, and I must say every time was a huge blessing for me. They came into my life and my journey; I can honestly say every single one of them gave me so much to help me in one way or another.

After the transplant, I vowed that anytime I could help anyone on their journey, I would so they would not have to do it alone like I did if that was what they wanted, I was there for them. I never would have gotten there without all the amazing Warrior Brothers and Sisters that helped me and stepped up for me.

I was thrown into a world I knew nothing about and somehow, I had to figure it out. Well, I will never say I got there by myself because that would be a flat out lie. Education is provided in the hospital for you, but so much is going on that a lot of it goes over your head.

Thankfully, I had people to talk to me after transplant about medicines, clinic visits, rejections, and finding my new normal. When you feel all alone in a battle and then someone comes along that has already been on that part of the road you are on and shares all they can, it makes all the difference in the world. Their insights and perspectives from another view are key to evolving into this life of transplantation. There is no better teacher to prepare you for the future than to watch one go through their own battles. I was a fighter before any connection I made or anything I learned from my Transplant Brothers and Sisters but seeing them do it for themselves was the greatest lesson. I have lost so many on my journey, but what I gained from them cannot be measured.

Someone can teach you to be tough and to be a fighter but doing it in the transplant world is a whole different ballgame, and I can only imagine that it may be similar to those battling terminal illnesses like cancer and other diseases. Seeing my peers' battle this way taught me so much that I was able to add to the strong foundation that my Momma and Dad helped me build early on in my life.

Even with all of that said, early on I had a lot to learn and not a lot of time to do it. All of these great Warriors are a direct result of where I am now and how I was able to get here. I watch countless times when Warriors would receive bad news, do it with a smile, and still give thanks for it. I have seen some do as I have and continue fighting after they have been given what I call the past due date. I say that because how does anybody really know how much time we have. I wish I could see those quitters faces now eight years later after telling me I had two months to live.

The will, determination, and fight in a Warrior can never be measured. I have seen my transplant brothers and sisters keep fighting even as they slip away more each day. I have seen them beat the odds for more time and the chance for more memories. I have seen them fight one obstacle after another just to get out of the hospital. I have seen them with PICC lines, ports, and tubes for all types of reasons. I have seen all of this every time I have looked in the mirror and with countless others, mainly my Lung Brothers and Sisters battling to stay alive before transplant and after rejections and hospitalizations, surgeries and rehabs. I have seen them everywhere. People often asked me, "How did you do it, Mark?

Well, I will tell you, I did many things I saw others do before me. I learned from the great Warriors and Mentors and my Lung Brothers and Sisters. The inspiration and motivation I got from so many has helped me to this point and the day I am in now, amazing as they all were. They became my family to love, to learn about, to lean on, to learn from, and to fight for and with. The only way I could repay that is to give as much back as I can.

If I have done that for someone, it is because another Warrior gave it to me. It is like passing a flame and everyone gets to start his or her own fire or add fuel to an ongoing fire. The day the quitters revealed themselves to me, I took that, put it in my fire, and used it for fuel as well.

Their word was not written in stone, and as far as I was concerned, they could take those two months and stick it where the sun doesn't shine. Even if I had only made it three months, I would still be a Warrior because that is what I am. That is what I do. They had no idea how many months I had. I have seen one warrior outlive, two separate past due dates of one month each, and for her, all I know is it has powered her to do great things. When we fight as Warriors, we also give others an opportunity to do the same with our example.

Backing words with action always does the best to show anyone they are equally capable of the same. Sometimes we show each other how to fight by fighting together; leading by example has always been great advice, especially if it came from someone who did so. The quitters told me two months, come on man! I was doing it one day at a time, and that is how we should always do it because that is the only way we can do it.

No matter if we are healthy or sick, rich or poor, we only get one day at a time. How do any of us know what will be happening two months from now? I certainly don't, and if a quitter tells me so, well they don't have much credibility with me, so I think we all know that, right?

I've seen Warriors of all kinds have all kinds of reactions after receiving bad news, but I never heard one say, 'why me?' When I am around Warriors or with them on the phone, I become a sponge. It is absolutely true that only iron sharpens iron. All Warriors fight differently and have different battles, so there is a lot to learn from them all.

I have seen some of the greatest ones come and go. As sad as those days are when they pass, I know I was blessed to be a witness. I always remind myself to do things big and small for my Transplant Brothers and Sisters because they cannot do it anymore and it is even more fun when I do things that they used to do and that they used to like to do. They may have gone on to the next phase of their journey, but they will forever be connected to my heart, and so I have tried to take a little part of all of them and make it part of me. That is what helps me cope and stay away from the *'will I be next'* game. I have seen them tirelessly continue to sign up as donors or be the ambassadors for the gift of life, spreading awareness and education. I have seen them talk and read their writings. I have seen how far reaching his or her impact was coming from not knowing anyone before transplant.

I sure have been blessed by the ones I did meet after transplant, not to mention the relationships I have with their families. These are some of the most special gifts I talk about that are wrapped up in the initial gift of life from our angel heroes. A true Warrior understands it is not only about what they can do for themselves, but about what they can provide for many others to reach the Warrior level as well. If we only do it for ourselves, how can we really be considered Warriors?

We get so much from others in so many ways fighting our battles. It only makes sense to send it down the line. That is how so many Warriors I have been blessed to be around have done it, and so I am fortunate to have had them as my example of how to do it.

When you see success in this world, you do what you can to duplicate it and use it to the best of your abilities. I have used some things others used with me and have had positive results just as we are all different.

I have seen Warriors fall repeatedly only to get back up and dust themselves off, to get back to fighting and making a difference, in not only one life, but also many lives, countless lives, but they started with their own. When we are knocked down and we are looking up more often than not, there is only one way to go. Most times when we get bad news, it is not the worst news we have could ever have. We find the self-discipline to fight on, doing what we do not want to as if we loved doing it the very most.

Repeatedly, self-discipline is just doing what we have to do to keep moving forward whether we want to or not, whether we like it or not. Doing all that is necessary to keep fighting our battles.

Everything is a battle to me because I rarely have anything in my life anymore that is not worth fighting for. We as Warriors have learned that cutting out that which is not necessary, or a waste of time and energy can only serve to weaken us or deter us from our reason and purpose. I have seen fellow Warriors go through it all with a smile and great attitude, and that lets everyone else know it is okay to do the same. It is okay to be uncomfortable. It is okay to face the hard things.

Do not get me wrong. We also go through hard times, dark times and low times, and it does have an effect, but the strongest ones find the other side and create a positive out of it all.

When the quitters told me I had two months, I was shocked initially, then angry. That quickly turned to, "Oh yeah, you think I am not worthy of fighting for! Well, all of you are no longer worthy of being part of my Warrior life, being part of my team, part of my fight and you are now excused!"

Moreover, as I left there, I was determined one day to show them all how very wrong they were. They thought they could turn a Warrior into a statistic because they were afraid to fight and wanted to steal my hope so it would go easier for them. I do not think so. If you are scared, then have the guts to admit it instead of trying to convince me to join your quitters club to make it easier on your conscience.

Not all Warriors are the same. That much I have learned being around so many great ones. Nevertheless, the quitters, they are all cut from the same weak cloth and that day in Colorado, the quitters revealed their true colors.

To me, mine were as vibrant, strong, and true as ever. I would have had more respect for them if they had just said they were scared or unsure and did not think they had the skillset to handle this.

Take ownership of your weaknesses. Do not project it onto others as if they do not have what it takes. So that day when I asked, "Which one of you did God call and say, I had two months to live," and they gave me their watered-down Kool-Aid without sugar version of an answer, I knew they were out of their element and their league.

Warriors do not project their faults or weaknesses onto others. They work to make them their strengths and that is what sets them apart. Warriors also win even on their day of passing. Their reward for being a true Warrior and faithful Warrior is going home where we all want to go someday. A Warrior gives up that role the second they decide to quit because Warriors, the real ones never will.

When the quitters brought themselves into the light to be seen, it was a sad and disgusting day, not for me, but for them. They now knew deep down inside who they were. They see it every time they look in the mirror. I could not believe I trusted them so much and thought that they had what it took to be with me on my journey. It was a shocker, but it was eye opening to the point that everyone from here on in would have to prove they belonged on my journey.

I learned a valuable lesson that day. Words that are not backed with action are merely a bowl of alphabet soup, a bunch of letters thrown together that do not mean anything. And when a quitter shows you their true self, believe them the first time, no need to give them five or six chances to show you who they truly are.

My St. Joe's family have showed me their true colors over and repeatedly. Even if it meant drawing a line in the sand with me, had I not chosen their game plan for me, I would not be here. Do not get me wrong. Every Warrior gets tired of most things, but they will never be too tired to fight for themselves or the ones they love.

I've seen them be told they have to lose weight or be listed only to go forward and lose that weight and then be delisted for one reason or another. For example, an infection or this or that. I have seen others have to gain weight. How do you gain weight when your body is not producing proper Oxygen? I've seen them battle to be told they have to get worse health wise to be considered only to fight harder in the middle of the decline to get there. I have seen them come from not being able to walk to eventually running. How do you measure perseverance or resilience? Overcoming the odds to continue a fight is one of the most empowering things we can do because after that, the odds, statistics, and averages just become numbers. Warriors run to the battle and never away. We do not say, oh, no, not again, or I cannot. They say, okay, let's do this. If you want to fight, pack a lunch because you will be all day trying. We are ready. Those kinds of things.

For me, the best part of being a Warrior is not my personal victories. The best part is showing someone they have what it takes to be every bit the Warrior like me and unlocking that power source and mindset to go forward to their unheard of and make it real. I know all my Warrior Brothers and Sisters that have passed showed up to their next stop on their journey as just that, the toughest and smartest Warriors, Life Warriors. So, when you are a Warrior, if you stay ready, you never have to worry about getting ready. Relying on other Warriors does not make you less of one, and you never know when one of the strongest will lean on you. It is as if a network and we can feed off each other's vibes and gain courage and knowledge amongst each other.

Do not get me wrong, I want to and love to inspire anytime I can, but I crave inspiration and constantly search for sources. What is funny is they usually find me first when I am not even expecting it. Those are the impactful ones, the ones that last and endure the battles. Being in the presence of other Warriors should never have you question your level or standing. Learn and teach to become better.

From what I have seen from the truest is they stay away from doubt and fear. They use courage and belief in themselves to complete their mission. In addition, most of the time that involves fighting and helping. As Warriors, we fight daily for every single day, and many times are thankful when God wakes us up in the middle of the night just to use the bathroom, our eyes open again. Who cares what the reason or what the time? They are open, we are alive, and the story continues. Another chance, another gift, another purpose. Because every day we wake up, God has a purpose for us here. God is not up there just waking up people making mistakes and waking up the wrong ones. So, if he wakes you up, do something purposeful. Always, every Warrior walks their path for a reason and fights for their purpose.

Chapter 21

Looking Back and Moving Forward

I have been on this transplant journey for over 12 years now, and most times when I look back, I have a hard time believing it. It still has me humbled beyond words, but realizing that now more than ever, none of this was possible without God. The things I have seen and the places I have come back from serve as reminders of how I have made it this far on this road. The faith and mental strength that it requires to be a Warrior can never be fully measured. Every Warrior has their last day on this battlefield and when that day comes, they have won all their battles, and their reward is to go home where we all want to go someday.

Warriors never lose because a true Warrior never quits and will always fight. A true Warrior fights to the last breath and does it all with courage and love. When I look at how many doctors gave up on me or never gave me a chance, they seem small, and the few that took a chance on me and fought for me, well, they appear grand and huge.

The quitters, I call them that because that is what they did to earn that moniker and the chances that they were familiar with that practice are very high. It is the ones that see there is not a chance but commit to the fight and go all in that are great. These are the great ones, the ones that matter, the ones that make a difference.

The first place I was at seemed like they enjoyed showing me off when I was fresh out, all sparkly, clean and new. However, when that faded, so did they. It was not all of them, but it was enough of them for me to know who they were.

Hanging banners that said how good they were according to US News and World Report and patting themselves on the back rather than fighting for the patients, the true reason why they should always fight. Some places are actually the best in the country, but you will not see advertising. You will not see bragging about their accomplishments. I pray that everyone finds the right place as I did after the wrong one was more than okay writing me off for dead. It truly makes all the difference in the world and your recovery and your progression.

There were a lot of people I will never forget because they gave me their best, but just as many that I cannot forget because what they gave me was their worst. They have earned the name I gave them: "The Quitters in Colorado" and they know who they are. When I went to St. Joe's in Phoenix, Arizona, in the state I was in, I would not have blamed them if they said no.

One Hundred and twenty pounds with a pulmonary embolism the size of a nickel and in a wheelchair. They did not though, and they jumped in the middle of my fight with both feet and never doubted their choice.

Every single person on the team was and always has been all in, and I cannot thank God enough for guiding me to the great place and these great people. Quitting always has that ugly negative blowback eventually, and I cannot imagine the feeling of doing that. The feeling of looking in the mirror. After they did that, how did they look at me and tell me there was nothing they could do for me? Did they think I wasn't worth fighting for? Were they more than concerned with their numbers so they could keep that ridiculous banner hanging up? US News World Report knows nothing of my fight and never will, so what do I care about some BS banner?

Nevertheless, all that fades and when I think about the great ones that knew nothing about me, only that I had quitters in charge of my care, they missed something big trying to protect their banners and then called it something else. As I look back, I realize I ended up in the right place, but I had to go through hell to get there. I had to walk through the fires to get to the good place. I was just thankful that my legs worked enough to keep on moving.

The things I have learned and those I have crossed pathways with on this journey are all blessings. What I have learned about myself is vast and very valuable going forward. I have much to look back on. That which was meant to kill me yet instead built and changed everything about me to get to this point was supposed to take place going forward. I have much to look back on. Everything about me is getting to this point.

Coming from this place of broken to the unheard of and everything in between. I have lived a life that is unbelievable and what it took me to progress to this level of Warrior. It has taken a lifetime of training and hitting walls only to find the strain to bust through them and thrive in a scary and unpredictable place, between all the ones made by doctors and me.

The mistakes along the way have all served as lessons. Most of them learned the hard way. They also serve to teach all what I will allow around me going forward for the rest of my days.

Someone once told me I could not do it, and I asked, "Why? Because you say so or because you know you can't?"

When you believe in yourself, you may be the only one that does, but you are the only one that matters. Also, that is how a great story starts with doubts and fears swirling everywhere. One belief is what gave a miracle the chance to become a story. Anyone can quit but not everybody does.

We have seen this repeatedly. It is important to not fall into that mindset and it's okay and it's easy to do just that. When we are tested, we begin to show ourselves our own true colors, but it also gives us an opportunity to change the ones we do not like or the ones we know are detrimental to us.

We never really know what we are made of or how far we can go till we are on that road being tested at every curve and turn. I never would have done any of this without God and awesome people around me courageous enough to take this journey with me. Even when I screwed up so badly, there were still those that stuck by me and believed as I did, that I could turn it around.

To all of those that stuck with me, helped me, inspired me, and prayed for me. I say I am eternally grateful, and for those who quit on me, turned their backs on me and threw dirt on my name, I also say thank you because that made me better too.

The most gratitude goes to God and my two ANGEL-HEROES. For without them I would have been gone long ago. Now, when I look back, I know I am going forward in a manner that shows my journey. Not everyone has walked through the fire and been able to leave some light along the way, but I am grateful that I have. I would not change a thing about all my struggles and battles because they have shaped me to be the Warrior I am today. All of this is the best thing that has ever happened to me, so if we ever meet or you hear my story, please do not say, 'I feel bad for you,' or 'I'm sorry this happened to you,' because I am not.

I am grateful for every single second of it, I always will be, and I will continue to show it by sharing, mentoring, praying, and helping until the day this Warrior is called home.

As I look at my journey from diagnosis to pre-transplant to transplant, post-transplant to my second transplant, to the return to my career and to the eventual, moving on to my new career, I have seen so many things. I have seen so many hard days, but I will tell you this, I have not seen very many days that I did not smile. I have seen even fewer days where I did not see positivity flowing. And I've even seen less than that where I didn't see change taking place from a stonemason, fighting for his life, fighting for his daughter, fighting for more time to moving into the space of being a public speaker and an author, and a transformational empowerment coach helping others fight for theirs.

In those 13 and a half years, I have healed. I have learned I have become better. I have become smarter. I have become stronger. However, in those 13 plus years, there have been days where I became weaker, where I became sick, where I became ignorant, where I was weakened beyond measure.

Also, it is only by the grace and mercy of God that I am able to sit here today and write a book, speak on stages, or help people by showing them what worked for me. For I truly was the mad scientist in the laboratory. But I was also the Guinea pig. And that was the only thing that was going to get me out of some of the darkest places my health challenges and my bad choices put me. However, when we begin to silence the negatives, starve our fears and doubts, and cease operating in self-sabotage, the changes that can take place are immeasurable. The power we can attain is indescribable, and the feats that we accomplish now, once seemed impossible, are now things that we believe that we can do normally, regularly, and impact others. So as I move into this new space in my life, I thank God for this opportunity to help people with my story, with my message of strong faith and resilience

With a love for life so strong, my persistence is what led to my perseverance in fighting in order to gain my life back. A life I never knew I could have and discover things about me that I never knew. I found things about me that could make a difference in this world, things that we all have within us. It is so true that God makes us in his image. We all have something in us put there from our Creator to make a positive and impactful difference in his world.

So, moving forward, I just challenge everybody out there to be fearless of doing the hard and challenging things. Believe in yourself so much that operating in self-sabotage is just out of the question, and to find your place of power and greatness that God has for you to do good, to impact the masses, and to spread the light that God has put inside of you everywhere you go. Also, that you may never take a step in your life where you are uncertain or walking in unbelief or where you are walking without purpose, for it is a very difficult and lonely place to walk.

When and if you are challenged with the greatest things in your life, do not cower, do not quit. If it seems as though God has filled your plate up with so much that you do not understand, please know that if God has put that much on your plate, that God has a confidence in you, that you are great, and that is why he gave you that. If God has that confidence in you, then you should have that confidence in yourself. Just always, know that no matter what God puts on your plate, God knows how big your plate is. So, knowing that God has that confidence in you, go out there and make your mark on the world. If you trip and fall, or if you flat out make a bad choice and mess up, own it, fix it, become better. When you make it right, that is how you become better. The measure of a man is not in his mistakes or his bad choices. The measure of that man is what he does after it. Does he point the finger, blame others, make excuses, or does he own it? Does he fix it and make it right? Does he learn from it so as not to repeat it? That is the measure of the man.

When you're in the toughest times of your life, just know that you have everything it takes to battle your way out of it and back into the light for if you didn't, God would not have placed you in that battle.

This book has shown me the possibilities are endless, but I never would have got here because in the beginning, I had no idea how much healing I needed. It was not until I was writing for a good amount of time that I realized that I had taken on excessive amounts of damage, that I needed a lot of work, and that I needed a lot of healing.

So, whether this book sells 1 copy, 10 copies, or 10 million copies, it is invaluable to me because it showed me how much I needed to heal and incentivized me to get that very healing that I needed in order to grow. Also to eventually level up so I can begin helping others who need the help and then they can begin to help themselves in this life. If you do not believe in yourself, nobody else will. If you do not fight for yourself, nobody will, your word, your fight, your love, your discipline, your integrity, your work ethic, your strength, all those things are only a matter of what you make them and what you put into them. Realize that all those words that were just said, there is a flip side to them.

When we do not create an environment to make those things stronger and stronger every single day, they become weaker. Every day is a gift. Do not ever forget it. The most challenging ones are the biggest gifts. A bad half hour or hour is not a bad day, a bad day is not a bad week, and a bad week is not a bad month. For every day, God gives you 86,400 seconds to do something with. If some of those seconds are messed up, it does not mean the other seconds do not have value. A flat tire does not equal a bad day. Not even walking out of a doctor's office after they told you that you had two months to live equals a bad day. You know why?

Because you walked out of that office, you were able to recognize the ones that did have what it took to be on that road with you on that journey, and you moved on that road on your own. Now, if that is not victory, I do not know what is. Since that day, I have experienced many victories. I have experienced setbacks. Do not get me wrong. Everybody has setbacks, everybody experiences defeat. The only time in life when you truly lose is when you quit. The rest of the time, you are just learning, or you are pivoting, or you are finding a different road to get to the greatness that God has for you. Do not ever forget that the only true losers in life are the quitters, because there is no coming back from that. Therefore, in life, when you are faced with your greatest struggles, your greatest battles, yes there will be fear. Yes, there might be doubt. Yes, it may look bleak; it may look like the unheard of, but guess what? After you take the first step, it is easier to take the second step and then the third. Then, before you know it, you can run right towards your battle, run through your battle, and to the next battle. Do not forget to make sure in between battles that you celebrate a little bit, rejuvenate, and restrengthen yourself and rest and refocus. Because a Warrior's battles never end. There is always another battle.

Until God calls you home, do not let the negative things in your life define you. Do not let somebody else tell you how tough you are, how strong you are, what you can or cannot do, or how faithful you are. Do not ignore your heart. Do not ignore your brain, do not ignore your body or your soul or you will fall.

Also, do not forget that if you feed them properly, they will always be ready and able to get you through anything, anytime, anyway, anyhow, anywhere, all day, every day. God does not make quitters and losers, but society does, and our bad habits, behaviors, and excuses do. God only makes Winners and Warriors. In conclusion I just want to say that somewhere down the road of life you will be hit hard by LIFE INTERRUPTED and when you do get knocked down as you are trying to get back on your feet I want that you remember me and my fight. Then I want you to say as you look in your mirror, "Well he got up and got back in his fight, Whats it going to be today? Are you going to stand up and fight like a Warrior or are you going to curl up in a ball in the corner and fell sorry for yourself and quit like a coward?"

NEVER QUIT ALWAYS FIGHT WHAT IS ON THE OTHER SIDE OF YOUR BATTLE IS YOUR GREATEST REWARD.

Mark Rodriguez

STAY BLESSED, STAY STRONG, STAY IN THE LIGHT, AND AS ALWAYS STAY IN YOUR FIGHT!

Me

www.ingramcontent.com/pod-product-compliance
Lightning Source LLC
Chambersburg PA
CBHW060134240125
20711CB00007B/1215